UNITED NATIONS CONFERENCE ON TRADE AND DEVELOPMENT

Practical Implementation of International Financial Reporting Standards: Lessons learned

Country case studies on
IFRS

UNITED NATIONS
New York and Geneva, 2008

NOTE

Symbols of United Nations documents are composed of capital letters combined with figures. Mention of such a symbol indicates a reference to a United Nations document.

The designations employed and the presentation of the material in this publication do not imply the expression of any opinion whatsoever on the part of the Secretariat of the United Nations concerning the legal status of any country, territory, city or area, or of its authorities, or concerning the delimitation of its frontiers or boundaries.

Material in this publication may be freely quoted or reprinted, but acknowledgement is requested, together with a reference to the document number. A copy of the publication containing the quotation or reprint should be sent to the UNCTAD secretariat at: Palais des Nations, CH-1211 Geneva 10, Switzerland.

UNCTAD/DIAE/ED/2008/1

UNITED NATIONS PUBLICATION
Sales No. E.08.II.D.25
ISBN No. 978-92-1-127571-1

no loan

UN2

TD/UNCTAD/DIAE/ED/2008/1

Preface

For over three decades, the United Nations has been contributing to the global efforts aimed at promoting transparent corporate accounting and reporting. The need for a global set of high-quality financial reporting standards has been apparent since the early 1970s. The existence of a global benchmark enables direct comparison of corporate financial reports between jurisdictions. Such high-quality standards enhance investor's confidence by allowing economic transactions of a similar nature to be treated and reflected in the same manner around the globe. What was only a vision three decades ago has now become a reality. As of the beginning of 2005, over 100 countries, including the European Union, either require or permit use of international financial reporting standards (IFRS) for preparation of financial statements by enterprises in their respective jurisdictions.

The full benefits of such a global benchmark will be realized only when it is implemented around the world in a consistent manner. Many developing countries and countries with economies in transition lack the accounting infrastructure and professional institutions needed for building the technical capacity required to meet the challenges posed by the transition to a common set of global standards – standards that are formulated with developed markets in mind and which have been becoming increasingly sophisticated.

In light of these important developments, UNCTAD's Intergovernmental Working Group of Experts on International Standards of Accounting and Reporting (ISAR) has been deliberating on practical challenges that arise in the implementation of IFRS. In particular, during the twenty-third and twenty-fourth sessions of ISAR, country case studies were discussed with a view to facilitating sharing of experiences and important lessons learned among member States.

This publication has been prepared to disseminate the lessons learned to a wider audience. As a growing number of developing countries and countries with economies in transition are embarking on the IFRS implementation process, the need for sharing experiences and lessons learned is becoming even more vital. It is my hope that policymakers, regulators, standard-setters and educators will find this publication to be a timely reference and a useful tool as they go about tackling practical implementation challenges of IFRS.

Supachai Panitchpakdi

Secretary-General of UNCTAD
August 2008

Acknowledgment

This publication was prepared by an UNCTAD team under the supervision of Tatiana Krylova, Head, Enterprise Development Branch; Nazha Bennabbes Taarji-Aschenbrenner, Officer-in-Charge, Enterprise Development Branch; and Dezider Stefunko, Officer-in-Charge, Accounting and Insurance Section. Yoseph Asmelash, Head, Accounting Unit, coordinated the research work in this area and prepared the manuscript for this publication. Anthony Miller provided valuable comments and suggestions. Peter Navarrette provided support in finalizing the manuscript for publication.

UNCTAD acknowledges with appreciation the contribution of the following in preparing the country case studies contained in this publication: Kati Beiersdorf and Kristina Schwedler, German Accounting Standards Board; Dennis Brown, Institute of Chartered Accountants of Jamaica; Caroline Kigen, Institute of Chartered Accountants of Kenya; Paulo R. Lustosa, University of Brazilia, Brazil; Shri Sunil H. Talati, Institute of Charted Accountants of India; Nazlı Ho al Akman, Professor, Bilkent, Turkey and Can Simga-Mugan, Professor, Middle East Technical University, Turkey; Mr. Syed Asad Ali Shah, Mr. Shahid Hussain and Ms. Maria Ahmed, from the Directorate of Technical Services of the Institute of Chartered Accountants of Pakistan; and the South African Institute of Chartered Accountants.

Executive summary

As of the beginning of 2005, the global corporate financial reporting landscape has been transformed in a major way – an unprecedented number of countries and enterprises around the world adopted international financial reporting standards (IFRS) as basis for the preparation of financial statements. All member States of the European Union have adopted IFRS endorsed in the European Union for the preparation of consolidated financial statements of listed companies in their respective jurisdictions. The benefits of a common set of high-quality financial reporting standards are very significant. Nevertheless, depending on the general economic situation, existing regulatory framework and financial reporting tradition of a given member State, practical implementation of IFRS poses considerable challenges. These practical challenges relate to the coherence of the regulatory framework and the state of preparation of relevant institutions, enforcement and technical capacity.

When IFRS are adopted in a given jurisdiction, they become part of existing laws and regulations. However, the provisions of relevant national laws and regulations might not be amended in due time to recognize the introduction of IFRS. In some cases, situations arise where IFRS requirements contradict applicable provisions in national laws and regulations. Relevant institutions needed for ensuring a smooth transition to a global set of financial reporting standards might be inexistent or weak. Rigorous enforcement of such global standards at the national level poses practical challenges due to absence of adequately resourced enforcement institutions and lack of adequate coordination mechanisms among relevant institutions.

Many member States, particularly developing countries and countries with economies in transition, lack a critical mass of competent accountants and auditors capable of applying highly sophisticated and voluminous global standards such as IFRS. In general, training materials on IFRS are scarce, particularly in languages other than English. Furthermore, proper application of certain measurement requirements in IFRS requires input from competent professionals in other areas such as actuary, property valuation and others. Lack of technical capacity poses a significant barrier to the successful implementation of IFRS.

Since 2005, UNCTAD's Intergovernmental Working Group of Experts on International Standards of Accounting and Reporting (ISAR) has been deliberating on practical implementation challenges of IFRS. The first chapter of this publication contains details of major practical implementation challenges and lessons learned from the experiences of members States that have embarked on the implementation process of IFRS. The remaining chapters, i.e., II–IX, contain country case studies of Brazil, Germany, India, Jamaica, Kenya, Pakistan, South Africa and Turkey.

Introduction

UNCTAD's Intergovernmental Working Group of Experts on International Standards of Accounting and Reporting (ISAR) has recognized the growing number of member States that are introducing international financial reporting standards (IFRS) as basis for the preparation of corporate financial reports by enterprises in their respective jurisdictions. In light of this development, the Group of Experts devoted substantial time during its recent sessions to deliberating on the practical challenges that arise in the implementation of IFRS. ISAR's deliberations on this topic at its twenty-third and twenty-fourth sessions were facilitated by a number of country case studies conducted in different regions of the world.

In concluding its twenty-fourth session, ISAR requested the UNCTAD secretariat to prepare a publication that synthesized the lessons learned in the practical implementation of IFRS by reviewing the country case studies that the Group of Experts discussed at its twenty-third and twenty-fourth sessions. Accordingly, the UNCTAD secretariat has prepared this publication. The remaining part of this section provides background information on ISAR's work in this area, with a view to providing readers with the context to this publication.

For over three decades, the United Nations has contributed to global efforts aimed at promoting comparable and reliable corporate reports. In 1973, the Secretary-General of the United Nations convened a group of eminent persons that recommended the creation of an internationally comparable system of standardized accounting and reporting. After a series of deliberations on this issue, the Economic and Social Council of the United Nations established the Intergovernmental Working Group of Experts on International Standards of Accounting and Reporting (ISAR) in October 1982 by resolution 1982/67.

Through ISAR, which is the only intergovernmental group at the international level that deals with corporate accounting and reporting, UNCTAD has contributed to the international debate on harmonization of accounting requirements, with a view to facilitating understanding of the implementation challenges faced by developing countries and countries with economies in transition. UNCTAD has assisted these countries in identifying and implementing internationally recognized good practices.

Many developing countries and countries with economies in transition strive to mobilize financial resources from domestic and international sources to attain their economic and social development goals. The availability of relevant information on potential investment targets has a bearing on efforts to mobilize investment for financing economic and social development. Such information plays an important role in making critical investment decisions and conducting risk assessment. It also contributes to improved investor confidence and decreased cost of capital. Over the years, attracting financing needed for economic development has become more competitive. Economic resources have become more mobile across borders. Enterprises that provide potential investors with reliable and comparable financial statements are more likely to attract domestic and international investment.

Recognizing the significant influence that corporate reporting has on investment decisions, developing countries and countries with economies in transition are attaching greater importance to transparency in corporate accounting and reporting. They are making efforts to strengthen the various components of the accounting infrastructure in their respective jurisdictions so that financial resources can be mobilized and used more efficiently. However, different countries have been using different national accounting standards, making it difficult and costly to compare investment opportunities in different countries. In addition, the faster pace of globalization, the growing interdependence of international financial markets and the increased mobility of capital have added to the pressure and demand for the harmonization of accounting and financial reporting frameworks and related standards around the world.

The need for a global set of high-quality financial reporting standards has long been apparent. The process of international convergence towards a global set of standards started in 1973 when 16 professional accountancy bodies from Australia, Canada, France, Germany, Japan, Mexico, the Netherlands, the United Kingdom and the United States of America agreed to form the International Accounting Standards Committee (IASC), which in 2001 was reorganized into the International Accounting Standards Board (IASB). The IASB develops global standards and related interpretations that are collectively known as international financial reporting standards (IFRS).

The process gained speed when the International Organization of Securities Commissions (IOSCO) endorsed the IASC standards for international listings in May 2000. It was further facilitated by a regulation approved in the European Union in 2002 required the preparation of consolidated (group) accounts of listed companies domiciled in the European Union in accordance with endorsed IFRS. Since then, many more countries have announced their plans to transition to IFRS, in some instances extending the scope of application beyond group accounts to legal entities and incorporating IFRS into their national regulatory frameworks.

At UNCTAD's tenth quadrennial conference in Bangkok, member States requested that the organization "promote increased transparency and disclosure by encouraging the use of internationally recognized accounting, reporting and auditing standards and improved corporate governance" (para. 122 of the Bangkok Plan of Action). At the eleventh conference in Sao Paulo, Brazil, member States reaffirmed the Bangkok Plan of Action and requested that UNCTAD "collect, analyse and disseminate data on best practices for stimulating enterprise development and identifying ways and means for enterprises, especially developing countries' SMEs, to meet international standards, including accounting standards" (para. 55 of the Sao Paulo Consensus).

At UNCTAD's twelfth quadrennial ministerial conference that took place in Accra in April 2008, member States called upon UNCTAD and ISAR to help developing countries and countries with economies in transition in building the necessary capacity and institutions needed for implementing international accounting and reporting standards and codes.

In October 2004, the twenty-first session of ISAR realized the international scope of the challenge of transition to IFRS and proposed to include this topic in its agenda for its twenty-second session. Accordingly, ISAR deliberated on the topic at its twenty-second session. In concluding its deliberations at its twenty-second session, ISAR reiterated the importance of a common set of principles-based and high-quality financial reporting standards, in support of the coherence and consistency of the international financial system for mobilization and efficient allocation of financial resources and for facilitating investment needed for the economic development of member States. Sound and internationally comparable corporate financial reporting that meets the requirements of financial markets improves investor confidence, facilitates risk assessment in making investment decisions, and helps reduce the cost of capital.

ISAR also recognized that, in order to reap the full benefits of harmonized global reporting standards and their consistent application in countries with different economic and business environments, a number of practical implementation challenges need to be addressed to assist developing countries and countries with economies in transition in meeting internationally recognized standards, particularly in the area of institutional and technical capacity-building.

The twenty-second session agreed on the need for conducting further reviews of the practical implementation challenges of IFRS, as well as ways to meet these challenges, including by preparing country case studies. One of the objectives of such reviews would be to identify good practices in IFRS implementation with a view to assisting policymakers, regulators and others in considering feasible implementation strategies to meet international standards in enterprise financial reporting and enhancing their input into the process of international convergence.

Accordingly, the UNCTAD secretariat prepared country case studies of Brazil, Germany, India, Kenya, and Jamaica. These studies were discussed at the twenty-third session of ISAR. After reviewing these country case studies, the twenty-third session of the Group of Experts reiterated the importance of principles-based, high-quality financial reporting standards, such as IFRS, for the coherent and efficient functioning of the international financial architecture, as well as the mobilization of financial resources for economic development. Participants at the session stressed the importance of a forum such as ISAR, where member States could share their views and experiences in this area, and identify best practices and guidance with a view to promoting harmonization, thereby facilitating the flow of investment.

In concluding its deliberations at the twenty-third session, the Group of Experts agreed to conduct additional studies and reviews to gain further insight into the challenges faced by developing countries and countries with economies in transition in meeting international requirements for high-quality standards. Accordingly, three country case studies covering Pakistan, South Africa and Turkey were prepared and considered by the twenty-fourth session of ISAR.

The main practical challenges that arise in implementing IFRS that have been identified through the country case studies discussed above and the lessons learned are presented in chapter I of this publication. It is important to note that although for the purpose of the country case studies efforts have been made to select countries in a manner that allows for coverage of diverse regions, economic systems and approaches to IFRS implementation, the case studies contained in this publication do not necessarily represent the whole range of issues in this area. An in-depth and detailed analysis of these issues could be a subject of further research and discussion.

Furthermore, the twenty-fourth session of ISAR has requested the UNCTAD secretariat to continue conducting studies on practical implementation issues relating to IFRS, including on related topics such as implementation of international standards on auditing (ISAs). Additional country case studies and other research in this area may be published in a subsequent volume.

CONTENT

Chapter I

Practical Implementation of International Financial Reporting Standards: Lessons learned

Overview of the country case studies

The country case studies cover Brazil, Germany, India, Jamaica, Kenya, Pakistan, South Africa and Turkey. These countries have taken a variety of approaches to implementing IFRS. In the case of Brazil, the implementation of IFRS will come into effect in 2010. German companies started preparing financial statements based on international accounting standards (IAS) beginning in the early 1990s. The approach in India has been to adapt IFRS to the economic realities of the country. Jamaica started implementing IFRS in 2002, while Kenya began the implementation process in 1998. Pakistan started introducing IAS issued by the International Accounting Standards Committee (the processor of the IASB) as early as in the 1970s. South Africa initiated a similar process in 1993. In Turkey, the process began in 2003.

The factors that initially contributed to the introduction of IFRS in the countries covered in the case studies vary. In Brazil, the Central Bank's intention is to bring financial reporting in line with international best practice to facilitate the comparability of financial reports and fostering investor confidence. In Germany, a number of large companies began to prepare their financial statements in accordance with IAS, not because they were required by national regulators, but in order to be able to access financial markets outside Germany. In 1998, German lawmakers gave listed companies the option of preparing their consolidated financial statements in accordance with IAS. The implementation of IFRS for the preparation of consolidated financial statements of listed companies in Germany became mandatory following the decision of the European Union to implement the IAS Regulation of 2002. The case study of Germany illustrates a European-Union-wide approach to implementing IFRS. Therefore, the implementation challenges extend beyond domestic factors.

The case study of Kenya shows a desire to raise national financial reporting requirements to international best practices in the aftermath of significant collapses in the country's financial services sector in the 1980s and 1990s. The case study of Kenya also indicates another factor that was taken into consideration in deciding to adopt IAS in place of national ones. By adopting IAS, the standard-setting body intended to reallocate resources away from setting national accounting standards to strengthening other activities aimed at more effective implementation of international accounting and auditing standards.

In India, the case study shows again a desire to harmonize domestic financial reporting requirements with international standards. However, in the case of India, yet another approach is taken, i.e., a programme of converging Indian accounting standards with IAS by adapting the latter to the economic reality of the country. The case study of Jamaica also cites an intention to harmonize corporate reporting practices across countries in the Caribbean in accordance with international requirements and with the position taken by IOSCO on its endorsement of IAS.

The case studies of Pakistan, South Africa and Turkey show that a desire to raise their financial reporting requirements to internationally recognized benchmarks is one of their main objectives in implementing IFRS. Furthermore, Turkey is negotiating membership with the European Union. The case study of Turkey illustrates the country's efforts to bring its financial reporting requirements in line with those of the European Union. The case study highlights the role of IFRS in facilitating economic integration on a regional basis.

In Pakistan, efforts are under way to bring the country into full compliance with IFRS by 2009. In the case of South Africa, while IFRS are adopted as they are issued by the IASB, a national-level due process is followed before an IFRS issued by the IASB takes effect in the country. In Turkey, although financial reporting standards applicable to companies whose shares are traded there are Turkish translations of IFRS, there are still certain differences between the two.

The extent of the application of IFRS in the countries included in the case studies varies from one country to another. As discussed earlier, in Brazil, financial institutions and listed companies are required to follow national standards that are gradually being converged with IFRS. In the case of Germany, listed companies are required to apply IFRS for preparing their consolidated financial statements. Non-listed companies are also allowed to use IFRS for the preparation of their group financial statements. However, both listed and non-listed companies are prohibited from using IFRS for preparing their individual (separate) financial statements. In Jamaica and Kenya, all listed and non-listed companies are required to prepare their financial statements – both consolidated and non-consolidated – in accordance with IFRS.

In India, there is a three-tier system of classification of entities (level I, II and III). Those in the first-tier are required to apply IFRS, as adapted for the country. The remaining two tiers are composed of small and medium-sized enterprises (SMEs). The reporting system allows certain simplifications and exceptions with respect to Level II and III entities.[1]

In Pakistan, there is a three-tiered approach, similar to the one adopted by ISAR. IFRS adopted in Pakistan are applicable to listed companies only. The Institute of Chartered Accountants of Pakistan has developed separate guidance on accounting and financial reporting for SMEs.

In South Africa, IFRS are applicable to listed companies whose shares are widely circulated. The country is considering recommending early adoption of draft IFRS for SMEs issued by the IASB in 2007 as a transitional measure. In Turkey, IFRS adopted in the country are applicable only to listed companies whose securities are widely held. The Turkish Accounting Standards Board has been working towards developing financial reporting guidance for SMEs, which is expected to be in line with the exposure draft of IFRS for SMEs issued by the IASB.

There are long-established laws and regulations governing corporate reporting, including parliamentary legislation on, among others, commercial codes and company acts. There are also a number of sector-specific regulations and institutions covering areas such as banking and insurance. For example, in Brazil, Germany and Turkey, regulation on corporate financial reporting is strongly linked to the legislative system. As a result, the introduction of new reporting systems or amendments to exiting ones requires significant consultation and processing through the legislative system. In the case studies of India, Jamaica, Kenya, Pakistan and South Africa, the professional accountancy bodies, i.e., the institutes of chartered accountants in India, Jamaica, Pakistan and South Africa and the Institute of Certified Public Accountants in Kenya play a central role in the setting of accounting standards or the implementation of IFRS and ISAs.

---

[1] This approach is similar to the one ISAR recommended in guidance on accounting and financial reporting for small and medium-sized enterprises (UNCTAD/ITE/TEB/2003/5 and UNCTAD/ITE/TEB/2003/6).

The legislative systems in these countries delegated the task of standard-setting in the areas of accounting and auditing to these private sector institutions. On the other hand, the case study of Turkey indicates that the Capital Markets Board and subsequently the Turkish Accounting Standards Board led the IFRS implementation process.

New German institutions have been established in recent years with significant responsibilities in the areas of corporate financial reporting. These are the German Accounting Standards Committee (and its standard-setting branch the German Accounting Standards Board), the German Financial Reporting Enforcement Panel and the Federal Financial Supervisory Authority. The latter two were established following the passing of the Accounting Enforcement Act of 2004. In Brazil, the proposed amendments to the current Corporate Act call for the establishment of a single entity responsible for preparing and issuing accounting standards.

In South Africa, the case study shows that the country envisages the establishment of a financial reporting investigation panel to improve the reliability of financial reports by investigating reported non-compliance with financial reporting standards and recommending measures for rectification or restitution. In the case of Pakistan, the Off-Site Supervision and Enforcement Department has been established to strengthen the enforcement activities of the State Bank of Pakistan.

These provide examples of the types of new institutional developments that are needed for the proper implementation and enforcement of IFRS.

The country case studies illustrate a number of practical challenges faced by these countries in implementing IFRS. These issues can be grouped into three main areas: institutional, enforcement and technical.

Institutional issues

When IFRS are introduced in a given jurisdiction, they form part of the pre-existing laws and regulations in the country pertaining to the governance of business entities. The case study of Jamaica shows a large number of regulatory institutions that have a bearing on the implementation of financial reporting standards. Often, laws and regulations overlap or become inconsistent with each other, especially when the roles and responsibilities of different institutions are not clearly defined and coordination mechanisms are not in place. Lack of coherence in the regulatory system becomes cause for serious misunderstandings and inefficiency in the implementation of IFRS.

As the case studies reflect, most of the laws and regulations pertaining to corporate reporting were enacted several decades before the introduction of IFRS. For example, the Companies Act of India passed into law in 1956. The foundations of financial reporting were formed in Pakistan by the Companies Ordinance of 1984, in South Africa by the 1973 Companies Act, and in Turkey by the Commercial Code of 1957. These laws remain in place without amendments to recognize the introduction of IFRS in the respective countries. As a result, the IFRS lack the necessary legal backing. For example, some company laws require specific formats for financial statements.

These requirements often contradict the ones in IAS 1 on presentation of financial statements. For example, IAS 1 specifically requires a cash flow statement. Such a situation impedes the smooth implementation of IFRS. In Pakistan, the Companies Ordinance of 1984 requires that surplus on revaluation of fixed assets be shown in the balance sheet after capital and reserves, whereas according to IAS 16 on property, plant and equipment, such surplus should be credited to equity under the heading of revaluation surplus.

In South Africa, the 1973 Companies Act requires that financial statements of companies must comply with generally accepted accounting practice. In 1992, an amendment to the 1973 Companies Act introduced the concept of statements of generally accepted accounting principles approved by the country's Accounting Principles Board as the basis for financial reporting.

In recognition of these contradictions, some countries have started introducing regulatory changes. For example, in Jamaica, the new Companies Act was passed in 2004, superseding the one from 1965. This new act does not specifically require compliance with IFRS; it states that companies should prepare their financial statements in accordance with the generally accepted accounting principles promulgated by the Institute of Chartered Accountants of Jamaica. In Brazil, a bill has been proposed to revise the Corporate Act which was passed by Congress in 1976.

In Pakistan, an example is the Finance Act of 2007, which amended section 248 (2) of the Companies Ordinance of 1984. In South Africa, the Corporate Law Amendments Act of 2006, which was issued in April 2007, is expected to be implemented in the near future. In Turkey, a new commercial code has been drafted and is awaiting enactment through the legislative process. Each of these legal reforms addresses aspects of IFRS in relation to the requirements of corporate financial reporting in the respective country.

The case study of India illustrates some approaches to giving the accounting standards issued by a professional body the necessary authoritative clarity and backing by various regulators. The Reserve Bank, the Securities and Exchange Board and the Insurance Regulatory and Development Authority specifically require compliance with the accounting standards issued by the Institute of Chartered Accountants of India. The same case study also illustrates the interactions between standard-setters, preparers and the courts when differences of opinion arise between standard-setters and preparers. For example, when the Institute of Chartered Accountants of India issued an accounting standard on leasing, based on the equivalent IAS, the Association of Leasing Companies approached the courts to seek relief from the standard, arguing that it was onerous for the leasing companies.

IFRS are intended to be used for the preparation of general-purpose financial statements. However, as the case studies show, IFRS-based financial statements could be also required to be prepared for statutory purposes as well. However, while extending the use of IFRS for such purposes might appear to be cost-efficient, it may create misunderstanding between reporting entities and regulators, particularly in situations where the regulator for a given sector has specific financial reporting requirements that differ from IFRS.

The regulatory bodies that put in place statutory financial reporting requirements on specific sectors include banking and insurance oversight authorities. For example, in Turkey, the Bank Regulation and Supervision Agency regulates financial institutions. This agency issued accounting standards that financial institutions under its supervision should follow. The case study of Pakistan provides an example where the regulatory agency for banks – the National Bank of Pakistan – prescribes formats for financial statements and other disclosures, which are not necessarily in conformity with IFRS. Similarly, in South Africa, prudential regulation of banks and insurance entities is conducted through laws that are distinct from the regulation of entities in other sectors.

The practical implementation issue that arises in this context is to what extent IFRS-based general-purpose financial statements could be used for prudential regulation. Such an

4

arrangement would require clear understanding to be reached among the different regulators. In the case study of Kenya, it can be seen that there is a lack of coordination between the Insurance Commissioner, who is responsible for the enforcement of the Insurance Act, and the Institute of Certified Public Accountants of Kenya, which has the responsibility to ensure that its members comply properly with implementing IFRS. Differences emerged due to differing requirements in IFRS 4 on insurance contracts and specific schedules required by the Insurance Commissioner. The Insurance Commissioner and the Institute of Certified Public Accountants of Kenya reached an agreement covering situations when the IFRS-based schedules differed from those required by the Insurance Commissioner, to the effect that a reconciliation certified by the auditor of the entity would be provided.

There are also further examples of inconsistencies between prudential regulation and IFRS-based measurement requirements. For instance, IFRS 4 on insurance contracts requires the percentage to be applied for calculating claims reserves on insurance contracts to be based on the past experience of the reporting entity in question. However, the prudential regulation on insurance would usually prescribe a predetermined percentage to be applied sector-wide, regardless of the prior experience of the entity in question. A similar situation arises with respect to provisioning for losses in the banking sector. Central banks often set a prescribed percentage amount that does not take into account the loss experience of the reporting entity as IFRS requirements would do.

Enforcement issues

One of the critical elements in the implementation of IFRS is the rigorous enforcement of standards. The full benefits of a global set of financial reporting standards such as IFRS will be realized only when these standards are consistently enforced. Thus, IFRS consist of only one element of the financial reporting infrastructure. The institutions responsible for enforcing IFRS need to realize that, as a result of the growing globalization of financial markets, their enforcement efforts often protect both domestic and international investors.

The responsibility of enforcing IFRS rests with a number of parties. Institutions such as securities exchange commissions, banking and insurance supervisory authorities, stock exchanges and capital market authorities play important roles in enforcing financial reporting requirements like IFRS.

As discussed earlier, the case study of Germany shows examples of additional institutions established in the country to ensure proper enforcement of IFRS. The German Accountancy Enforcement Act of 2004 established a two-tier enforcement mechanism. The first-tier is the German Financial Reporting Enforcement Panel composed of fifteen professional and industry associations. The second-tier in the mechanism is the Federal Financial Supervisory Authority. The Financial Reporting Enforcement Panel examines both consolidated and non-consolidated financial statements of entities listed in Germany. If the panel discovers violations that cannot be resolved with the entity examined, it refers the case to the Federal Financial Supervisory Authority. Listed entities in Germany make financial contributions to cover the costs of the Financial Reporting Enforcement Panel. An interesting aspect of such an institutional arrangement is that it makes use of the extensive technical expertise that resides with private sector bodies, while retaining the enforcement responsibility with the government entity, in this case the Federal Financial Supervisory Authority.

The case study of India also shows how the professional accountancy body, i.e. the Institute of Chartered Accountants of India, plays a positive role in strengthening the financial reporting practices of entities in India. The institute established the Financial Reporting Review Board. The board selects and reviews financial statements of various entities to ensure that, among other things, the entities comply with accounting standards. In situations where the board identifies lack of compliance with accounting standards and other applicable standards and codes, it advises the Institute of Chartered Accountants of India and/or refers the case to the appropriate authorities for action.

The case studies illustrate various aspects of enforcing IFRS in the respective jurisdictions. In Pakistan, the Monitoring and Enforcement Department of the Securities and Exchange Commission of Pakistan is responsible for enforcing compliance with IFRS through regular review of the quarterly and annual financial statements published and filed with the commission by listed companies. In instances where it finds deficiencies or non-compliance with IFRS, it imposes fines and penalties on the preparers and their auditors.

In South Africa, the Generally Accepted Accounting Principles (GAAP) Monitoring Panel, which was created by the South African Institute of Chartered Accountants and the Johannesburg Stock Exchange in 2002, is responsible for ensuring compliance with financial reporting standards. Prior to the creation of the panel, there was no regulatory enforcement of financial reporting standards. In Turkey, the Capital Markets Board is responsible for monitoring and enforcing listed companies' compliance with financial reporting standards.

The case study of South Africa provides an example of how the GAAP Monitoring Panel dealt with the cases of financial reporting referred to it. Decisions that the panel took included withdrawal and reissuing of financial statements, suspension of listing and prospective application of amended accounting policies. Other cases were either pending or required no action.

One of the common aspects of the countries covered in the case studies is that most of them require an audit of IFRS financial statements to be conducted in accordance with ISAs issued by the International Auditing and Assurance Standards Board of (IAASB) of the International Federation of Accountants. Pakistan, South Africa and Turkey are in the process of implementing ISAs issued by the IAASB. The Brazilian convergence programme also envisages the implementation of IFRS and ISAs by 2010.

The Basel-based Financial Stability Forum has recognized ISAs as one of the twelve core sets of standards (which also include IFRS) which are needed to ensure the financial stability of countries around the world. Thus, coupling the implementation of IFRS with that of ISAs helps to raise the quality of financial reporting and auditing to the level of international best practice. ISAs are an important tool in enforcing the proper implementation of IFRS.

Professional accountancy bodies also play a role in the enforcement of IFRS as they discharge their responsibilities with respect to ensuring adherence to their membership by-laws. The case studies of India and Kenya provide examples of peer-review programmes that the respective professional accountancy bodies in these countries introduced to ensure proper implementation of financial reporting and auditing standards. In Pakistan, the Securities and Exchange Commission chartered accountants it finds to be at fault refers to the Institute of Chartered Accountants of Pakistan. The case study indicated that the Investigations Committee of the institute had received 20 disciplinary cases of its members and the committee dealt with 10 of them, including by suspending membership and referring the case to the courts.

Technical issues

Practical implementation of IFRS requires adequate technical capacity among preparers, auditors, users and regulatory authorities. Countries that implement IFRS face a variety of capacity-related issues, depending on the approach they take. The case studies illustrate a number of technical challenges in the practical implementation of IFRS. The concurrent implementation of IFRS and ISAs further compounds the difficulties. One of the principal difficulties encountered in the practical implementation process is the shortage of accountants and auditors who are technically competent in implementing IFRS and ISAs.

Usually, the time between when a decision is made to implement the standards and the actual implementation date is not sufficiently long to train a sufficient number of professionals who could competently apply international standards. For example, the case study of Kenya shows that the decision to implement IAS and ISAs effective in 1999 was actually made in 1998. The case study of Kenya further shows that there is still shortage of professional accountants, particularly those who are adequately trained on IFRS and ISA implementation. In general, while training on IFRS was needed in all countries covered by the case studies, the need appeared to be most pressing in the case of Turkey.

A related technical problem is the limited availability of training materials and experts on IFRS at an affordable cost. The case study of Kenya shows the challenges that the Institute of Certified Public Accountants of Kenya faces in this respect. The difficulty is further complicated in countries where training materials on IFRS that are currently available in English are not readily usable because of language barriers. The case studies of Brazil and Turkey highlight this issue. In Turkey, one of the capacity-building requirements is therefore translating IFRS into Turkish in a consistent and efficient manner.

Another technical challenge occurring after completing the initial implementation process is the difficulty in coping with the rapid frequency and volume of changes made by the IASB to existing IFRS, as well as keeping pace with new standards. A particular example highlighted in the case studies of India and Kenya is the IASB decision to amend 13 standards at the same time as part of its improvements project. As a result, more than 20 standards were affected because of the consequential amendments that were made. Repeated amendments on IFRS place strain on available technical capacity, which in many cases was already insufficient.

Frequent amendments to IFRS create further technical challenges in countries where amendments to IFRS take effect after going through due process at a regional or national level, as well as in countries where translation of the amendments is required. In the respect, the Institute of Chartered Accountants of Pakistan has adopted a policy to the effect that once an IFRS is adopted by the institute and endorsed by the Securities and Exchange Commission of Pakistan, any subsequent revisions or confirming amendments the IASB makes on the standard are considered as adopted, unless otherwise specified.

Fair-value measurement requirements in IFRS pose yet another significant technical implementation challenge. In particular, the case studies of India and Kenya indicate that where trading volume is low and capital markets are not sufficiently liquid, obtaining reliable fair value for IFRS measurement purposes becomes difficult. Preparers face difficulty in obtaining reliable measures of and data for, among others: discount rates in a volatile financial environment, cash-flow trends, crop yields, loan yields, loan default rates and sector-wide benchmarks for determining fair value for some items. The technical difficulties discussed above pose challenges to auditors too, as they need to assess the reliability of fair value measurements contained in the financial statements.

As the case study of South Africa shows, the computation of loan loss provisions for doubtful debts could create certain inconsistencies if appropriate clarification is not provided on how preparers should follow the requirements in IAS 39 as they transition from previous requirements, such as schedules provided by a regulatory body; in this case, the Central Bank.

In Pakistan, as a result of capacity limitations in the banking sector, the implementation of IAS 39 on measurement and recognition of financial instruments had to be done gradually. In South Africa, there are technical challenges to applying fair value-based measurements to financial instruments for which there is no active market or where the market was illiquid, and in circumstances under which management estimations are needed.

There are also regulatory complications that arise when fair value requirements in accordance with IFRS are applied in certain circumstances. For example, when life insurance contracts are unbundled in accordance with IFRS 4, gains on the investment (deposit) component of the life insurance contract are recognized on a fair value basis. However, insurance regulators might decide not to accept such gains as a part of profits available for distribution to shareholders.

The case study of Germany shows that the basis for classification of financial instruments either as equity or debt in accordance with IAS 32 differs from the requirements in German GAAP and law. When classified in accordance with IAS 32, certain instruments that would normally be classified as equity under German GAAP would be categorized as liability. This is mainly due to the right granted under German law to certain shareholders, such as private partnerships, to put back their shares to the entity. The result is a significant shift of equity to liabilities in a balance sheet prepared under IFRS. The legal form of a partnership is common in Germany and such partnerships are often subsidiaries of listed companies that are required to apply IFRS. As the case study indicates, the reduction in equity discourages many German entities from adopting the option of preparing their financial statements in accordance with IFRS.

The case studies reveal the difficulties encountered in implementing IAS 17 on leases, particularly among entities such as banks and insurance companies that would be required to re-classify certain leaseholds as operating leases to comply with the standard. The impact of this re-classification on banks and insurance companies was a reduction of capital with serious implications on capital adequacy requirements.

The case study on Kenya gives examples of situations where financial institutions had to dispose of non-core assets such as leasehold land and buildings that were held as investments. The Association of Leasing Companies in India challenged the Indian standard on leasing – which is based on IAS 17 – in the domestic courts. In the case study of Pakistan, the Institute of Chartered Accountants of Pakistan decided to defer application of Interpretation 4 of the International Financial Reporting Interpretations Committee (IFRIC) – determining whether an arrangement contains a lease – to 2009 as a result of concerns that application of IFRIC 4 would in effect convert independent power producers in the country into leasing companies.

The case study of South Africa illustrates yet another example of how national practice in the area of operating leases was amended to make it consistent with IFRS. Prior practice with respect to operating lease agreements with inflation escalations took into account the impact of inflation, and lease payments were computed and accounted for accordingly. After seeking the necessary clarification from IFRIC and realizing that what needed to be taken into account was not inflation, but rather factors that impact on the physical usage of the asset leased, the South African Institute of Chartered Accountants issued a circular to bring national practice on a par with IFRS.

Implementing the requirements on recognition of deferred tax liability for taxable temporary differences set by IAS 12 on income taxes seems to be another area where preparers are experiencing difficulties in complying with the requirements. The case study in India indicates that Indian Accounting Standard 22 – the IAS 12 equivalent that is supposed to introduce the concept of deferred taxes in India for the first time – is being challenged by preparers in the courts.

IAS 16 on property, plant and equipment takes the components approach to depreciating assets. Thus, each part of a tangible fixed asset is to be separately depreciated. This approach might be new to various preparers whose previous basis of financial reporting did not require a components approach. A technical issue that might need further guidance in this area is the extent to which preparers need to continue breaking a fixed asset into its various components for depreciation purposes.

The complexity of certain IFRS and the need for estimating certain elements of the financial statements require expertise beyond those issues that would normally fall within the domain of professional accountants and auditors in developing counties. For example, IAS 19 on employee benefits requires actuarial valuation to measure the obligations of a reporting entity. This valuation requires input from professional actuaries on a regular basis. The availability of qualified actuaries is critical in this context. Furthermore, there may be a need for coordination between the professional bodies of accountants and actuaries, with a view to reaching agreements on how estimations are to be conducted and the nature of details to be provided by the actuary. The case study of India provides an example where the Institute of Charted Accountants of India and the Actuarial Society of India worked together to ensure that the actuaries' reports contained the details required in IAS 19.

The case studies of South Africa and Turkey illustrate certain technical challenges that are specific to a given economy. In South Africa, implementation of the "Black Economic Empowerment" initiative brought about a need for technical clarification of accounting for the discount on equity instruments granted to black South Africans or entities controlled by them. The issue of whether to capitalize the amount of the discount granted as intangible asset or expense was brought to the International Financial Reporting Interpretations Committee (IFRIC). The issue was resolved when IFRIC issued IFRIC 8 – Scope of IFRS 2. South African companies that encounter transactions of this nature now treat discounts (on equity instruments granted) as expenses.

In recent years, the Turkish economy has experienced significant inflation. When an economy undergoes hyperinflationary situations, IAS 29 on financial reporting in hyperinflationary economies becomes applicable. In Turkey, however, the provisions of IAS 29 were not applied in full. Financial statements are prepared on historical-cost basis, with the exception of revaluation of property, plant and equipment.

Another technical implementation challenge discussed in the case study of South Africa pertains to accounting for certain investments in shares of parent companies by subsidiaries in the insurance sector. In certain situations, subsidiaries of insurance companies invest in shares of their holding companies. Such arrangements create a situation where investments would be considered as liability in the financial statements of the parent company. At the same time, these would also be considered as treasury shares and would be deducted from equity.

Lessons learned

In general, a review of the case studies shows that there is growing appreciation of the usefulness of IFRS by countries in different regions of the world irrespective of the size of their economies or financial reporting traditions. However, there are serious institutional, enforcement and technical challenges that countries need to overcome in order to benefit fully from the introduction of IFRS in their jurisdictions.

The transition plan to IFRS and its implications for preparers, users, educators and other stakeholders has to be effectively coordinated and communicated. Preparers, users, regulators, professional accountancy bodies and educators need to be engaged in the planning of IFRS, as well as the implementation. A country's transition action plan to IFRS needs to have a logistical framework of targeted activities to be completed within a specified period of time. The communication programme could include elements such as road shows to present the objectives of the transition to IFRS, raising the awareness regulatory bodies of the potential impact of the conversion, identifying regulatory synergies to be derived and communicating to preparers and users the potential temporary impact of the transition on business performance and financial position.

The implementation of IFRS requires considerable preparation both at the country and entity levels. One of the critical considerations is the need for ensuring coherence in the regulatory framework and for providing clarity on the authority that IFRS will have in relation to other existing national laws. Undertaking the necessary tasks to ensure coherence and clarity will require considerable resources and time.

The case study of Germany shows that entities need an average preparation period of between 12 and 18 months. The case study of South Africa provides findings of surveys carried out in 2005 and 2006 by the accountancy firm Ernst & Young on the preparedness of entities to implement IFRS. The case study of Turkey also discusses findings of a similar survey. These surveys indicate that implementation of IFRS is a complex process that requires extensive preparations. Thus, an IFRS implementation plan needs to take into account the time and resources needed for efficient and effective implementation at the entity level. The cost of staff training, updating information technology systems and arranging for external advice in preparation for the implementation of IFRS could be significant and needs adequate consideration. Entities in countries where there is a need to translate IFRS from English into another language might need a considerably longer period of time to be ready to make the transition to IFRS.

The transition plan needs to define the scope of application of IFRS clearly with respect to the size and type of entities, as well as defining clearly whether IFRS will apply for the preparation of consolidated and separate financial statements. The case studies show that SMEs encounter serious difficulties when they are required to apply IFRS to prepare their general-purpose financial statements. Therefore, prior to the transition to IFRS, a reporting regime for SMEs needs to be in place. It should also be clearly communicated to preparers and users. As the case studies of India and Pakistan indicate, a three-tier approach could be used: a first tier to apply IFRS, a second tier to apply IFRS-based standards adapted for that particular tier; and a third tier consisting of microentities applying a highly simplified system that is close to cash-based accounting.

Certain national financial reporting systems are traditionally integrated to serve general-purpose and some special-purpose reporting needs such as taxation and dividend distribution, as the case studies of Brazil and Germany illustrate. While the IFRS financial reporting model is designed to serve a range of accounting models, it might not be easily adapted to meet special-purpose reporting requirements in line with the traditional emphasis of the financial reporting system in a country; for example, creditor protection and capital maintenance in the case of Germany. As can be observed in the case study of Germany, both listed and non-listed companies are prohibited from using IFRS for preparing their separate (individual) financial reports.

Certain countries that make the transition to IFRS might need special consideration if their economies experience hyperinflationary situations. As indicated in the IASB Framework for the Preparation and Presentation of Financial Statements,[2] such countries might be able to specify a financial reporting model that is suitable for their specific circumstances through consultations with the IASB. Thus, in addition to the general implementation that transition to IFRS implies, countries with hyperinflationary currencies need additional considerations.

An IFRS implementation programme needs to adequately assess the state of readiness of relevant professional accountancy organizations so that the necessary resources are available to ensure competent and continuous support from such organizations. Successful implementation of IFRS needs extensive and ongoing support from professional accountancy associations. The role of professional accountancy organizations in implementing IFRS has been highlighted in the case studies. These organizations play an important role in building the technical capacity required for implementing IFRS in a sustainable manner. In the initial phase of implementation of IFRS, professional accountancy bodies contribute to technical capacity-building by providing training on IFRS to their members. Furthermore, professional accountancy organizations also facilitate training geared towards keeping their members updated on new technical developments in the area of IFRS.

In this respect, it is also important to recognize the importance of standards issued by the International Accounting Education Standards Board (IAESB) of IFAC which address various aspects of pre- and post-qualification requirements and continuing professional development.[3] The model accountancy curriculum, adopted by ISAR in 1999 and updated and revised in 2003, is another resource that could be useful in aligning national qualification requirements with international standards and guidelines.[4]

As part of the implementation strategy of IFRS, professional accountancy bodies could establish task forces or response teams that would reply to queries from members on IFRS and ISA implementation issues. Such a structure could be in place at the earlier implementation phase and could also be reconstituted at later stages in response to the issuance of new standards or amendments that require extensive elaboration for preparers and auditors to apply.

The case studies illustrate how professional accountancy bodies facilitate communication between the national professional accountancy body and other stakeholders on the one hand and the IASB on the other. Furthermore, such organizations contribute to promoting regulatory coherence on IFRS implementation by working closely with various national regulators and resolving practical implementation issues that arise when introducing IFRS.

---

[2] This issue is addressed in para. 110 of the IASB Framework for the Preparation of Financial Statements.
[3] Further information on the IAESB is available at www.ifac.org/Education/.
[4] UNCTAD, *International Accounting and Reporting Issues - 2003 Review*, pp. 200-257.

The case study of Kenya describes an annual award programme whereby the Institute of Certified Public Accountants of Kenya selects and recognizes the entities that ranked highest in preparing their financial statements in accordance with IFRS. Candidates submit their financial statements for review on a voluntary basis. Such an award programme encourages improved implementation of IFRS. At the same time, it provides the institute with valuable information on the particular areas of IFRS that preparers frequently have difficulty implementing, and which could be the subjects of future programmes of continuing professional education and other training events.

The case studies show how professional accountancy bodies contribute to the effective implementation of IFRS and ISAs through requirements that hold their members responsible for observing due care in implementing these standards.

Peer review programmes among auditors are a useful oversight mechanism and provide information on difficulties encountered in the financial reporting and/or audit process. Implementation difficulties that frequently arise in the findings of peer reviews provide useful feedback on where further education programmes need to focus. In those cases where challenges are sector-specific, more focused training programmes and additional resources (such as sample audit files) could be prepared by the relevant professional association or responsible regulatory body.

National accountancy firms could contribute to consistent application of IFRS, not only at the national level but also globally. The case study of South Africa illustrates how the Technical Partners Forum of accountancy firms in the country identifies technical financial reporting issues that require clarification in order to avoid inconsistencies. Members of this forum benefit from their international networks. This approach facilitates technical dialogue among accountancy firms at the national and international level, and promotes consistent application of IFRS.

Professional accountancy bodies, preparers and users, including regulators, could provide the IASB with useful feedback, not only after standards are finalized and ready for implementation, but early in the drafting process. The case studies show that, while some professional bodies and national accounting standard-setters are in a position to interact directly or indirectly (on a regional basis) with the IASB, others are not – mainly because of a lack of resources. One of the approaches suggested in the case studies is to develop a coordination mechanism at a regional level, so that, by pooling resources, countries are able to provide input to the standard-setting process as from the early stages.

The case study of South Africa provides a good example of how the South African Accounting Practices Committee promotes participation of the stakeholders in the country in providing input into the IASB standard-setting process. An exposure draft issued by the IASB is also simultaneously issued in South Africa for comment by the committee. The input received on the exposure draft issued in South Africa is considered by the South African Institute of Chartered Accountants when drafting its response on the exposure draft to the IASB. Proactive engagement with the IASB in the early stages of the standard-setting process, particularly on practical implementation issues of IFRS, could contribute to reducing requests for clarifications or interpretations after the standard is issued.

Integrating IFRS and ISA modules into university accountancy education curricula and coordinating university accountancy education programmes with professional qualification and regulation could contribute positively to the smooth implementation of IFRS in an economy. Lack of coordination in this area could lead to inefficient management of financial and human resources, especially in situations where university programmes are supported by local or national governments as part of national human-resources-development programmes.

The shortage of expertise in the field of IFRS affects not only the private sector, but also regulators and other government agencies. Therefore, to discharge their oversight responsibilities effectively, such agencies need to assess their needs for expertise in IFRS early enough in the implementation process and accordingly establish a human-resources-development programme. As IFRS change as a result amendments to existing standards or new standards being issued, regulatory agencies need to have a plan in place to keep up with the changes. Part of the plan needs to include continuing education programmes for personnel in charge of reviewing IFRS-based statements for regulatory purposes. The case studies provide useful examples of how regulatory agencies could benefit from expertise that resides with the private sector, including with preparers and auditors, by creating a mechanism whereby regulators receive technical advice, but maintain the regulatory decisions with the government oversight body.

Transitioning from national financial reporting standards to IFRS has the potential to create a need for clarification or interpretation of the provisions of certain IFRS in relation to certain country-specific circumstances. The case study of South Africa shows how such issues could be resolved by active engagement with IFRIC. While the majority of issues that require clarification or interpretation could pertain to situations that could be applicable to all jurisdictions, certain issues such as black economic empowerment are specific to a country. It is important to work closely with IFRIC rather than create a local interpretation which could lead to divergence of practice.

Discrepancies between IFRS that are in effect at the international level and those adopted at the national level should be avoided. The case studies illustrate the different approaches that countries have taken towards implementation of IFRS. Certain countries require either an additional due process to be followed at a national level or a translation into a national language to be done before IFRS become effective. These requirements often cover newly issued IFRS and interpretations or amendments. These requirements for additional steps could create discrepancies between the body of IFRS issued by the IASB that are in effect at a certain time and IFRS required at the national level. Users, particularly those outside the country, might find that such discrepancies create barriers to direct comparison of financial reports on a global basis. Thus, member States need to pay particular attention to the undesirable effects of any discrepancies that could be introduced by the approach they choose.

Unlike countries that implement IFRS, those that have chosen to adapt IFRS to their specific circumstances have more flexibility with respect to issuing additional interpretation and guidance on the IFRS equivalents which are deemed to apply to their economies. As shown in the case study of India, the Institute of Chartered Accountants of India issues various interpretations and guidance on the IFRS adapted to the economic environment of India. However, interpretation or guidance that diverges from the general thrust of IFRS might defeat the purpose of adapting IFRS in the first place, particularly if the objective is to ultimately comply with IFRS as issued by the IASB. This is especially relevant when considering that the IASB does not allow any further guidance or interpretation other than the implementation guidance it issues or the interpretations issued by IFRIC.

Enforcement authorities play a positive role in consistent implementation of IFRS by facilitating sharing of enforcement decisions. The case studies provide good examples of how enforcement authorities, such as securities and exchange commissions and financial reporting monitoring panels, could contribute to more consistent application of IFRS by sharing their findings and enforcement decisions, with a view to helping preparers to avoid incorrect application of IFRS by allowing them to learn from the experience of other preparers.

International and regional development banks play a positive role in implementation of IFRS by providing resources to developing countries and countries with economies in transition. The case studies indicate that substantial financial support is needed to achieve the goal of IFRS implementation. International and regional development banks can provide assistance in overcoming the implementation challenges faced by developing countries in implementing IFRS. As the case study of Jamaica indicates, subsequent to the decision of the Institute of Chartered Accountants of Jamaica to implement IFRS, the World Bank conducted an assessment of the implementation of accounting and auditing standards as part of a programme to determine the gaps in standards and compliance. This was carried out as part of the World Bank Reports on the Observance of Standards and Codes initiative. The Inter-American Development Bank provided financial support for the Institute of Charted Accountants of Jamaica, which took the form of technical cooperation to disseminate information on IFRS, training and outreach, building enforcement and compliance capabilities, and establishing sustainable training programmes.

Chapter II

Case study of Brazil

I. Introduction[1]

In 2004, the Brazilian economy experienced significant growth, with the country's gross domestic product (GDP) growing by 5.2 per cent – the highest growth rate since 1994.[2] Brazil attracted close to $18 billion in foreign direct investment (FDI). At the same time, outward investment from Brazil amounted to $9.5 billion.[3] As of June 2006, there were 31 Brazilian companies listed on the New York Stock Exchange. Integrating into global capital markets and facilitating the mobilization of capital and fostering investor confidence call for national corporate transparency requirements which are consistent with international best practices, including in the area of corporate financial reporting. These trends have underpinned efforts aimed at converging national accounting and reporting standards to International Financial Reporting Standards (IFRS) in Brazil. To this end, various reforms in the area of accounting are being undertaken in the country.

At present, Brazil is gradually converging its accounting standards and the International Financial Reporting Standards (IFRS) issued by the International Accounting Standards Board (IASB). The main institutions leading the convergence process are the Brazilian Securities Commission (CVM), the Brazilian Institute of Independent Auditors (IBRACON) and the Central Bank of Brazil.

A number of developments have recently advanced the country's progress towards IFRS. In March 2006, the Central Bank of Brazil announced that, as of 2010, all financial institutions under its supervision will be required to prepare their consolidated financial statements in accordance with IFRS. The Brazilian Securities and Exchange Commission has promoted efforts by companies listed in capital markets in Brazil to gradually adopt IFRS. For example, the CVM has been working more closely with IBRACON to accelerate convergence with IFRS. Companies listed on Sao Paulo Stock Exchange's New Market (launched in December 2000) are required to provide financial statements prepared in accordance with IFRS or to the United States generally accepted accounting principles (GAAP), in addition to those that are prepared under Brazilian accounting standards. The Committee of Accounting Pronouncements was recently set up in Brazil, whose declared objective will be to achieve full adoption of IFRS in the country.

However, despite the significant changes that have occurred in the Brazilian accounting system in recent years, there are still important differences between Brazilian accounting standards and IFRS. Some practical and operational factors, such as the legal environment and economic, tax, cultural and educational issues, tend to place obstacles in the path of convergence of Brazilian accounting standards and IFRS. Economic and tax issues particularly affect the process of convergence of Brazilian accounting and IFRS, because the accounting system in

---

[1] This chapter was prepared and edited by the UNCTAD secretariat based on significant inputs provided by Professors Paulo Roberto B. Lustosa, Jorge Katsumi Niyama, Ducineli Régis Botelho de Aquino (all at the University of Brasilia, Brazil).

[2] Central Bank of Brazil, *Annual Report 2004.*

[3] UNCTAD *World Investment Report 2005*, pp. 64-66.

Brazil is strongly tied to tax laws and regulations that establish rules for recognition, measurement and disclosure of business transactions.

This chapter provides a brief overview on the development of accounting systems in Brazil and its current status, discusses the salient features of regulatory frameworks and enforcement, outlines some of remaining major differences of accounting rules in Brazil with regard to IFRS and summarizes main lessons learned through the recent process of reforming of accounting system to conform to IFRS.

II. Regulatory framework and enforcement

The accounting system of Brazil was initially developed under the influence of European countries (mainly Italy) and was later affected by United States accounting practices. It is strongly influenced by the country's tax legislation, corporate laws and rules established by government agencies. These agencies include a number of organizations such as the Central Bank of Brazil, the Brazilian Securities Commission (CVM), the Superintendence of Private Insurance, the National Telecommunications Agency and the Secretariat for Complementary Pension Funds.

The stock market and national financial system reforms in the 1970s underpinned the development of accounting in the country. In 1976, the CVM was created to supervise the stock market and regulate the establishment of accounting standards for listed companies.

Reforms of the financial system included measures such as the requirements for listed companies to have their financial statements audited by independent auditors and comply with the financial reporting standards issued by the Central Bank of Brazil under instruction No. 179/72. Another measure included the introduction of the Corporate Act (No. 6.404/76), which included specifications on accounting principles that companies were required to apply. It also established recognition and measurement criteria and accounting procedures that were strongly influenced by the United States GAAP. Prior to the 1970s, Brazilian accounting was strongly influenced by tax legislation.

With regard to the regulatory framework, Brazilian companies can be classified as: (1) companies listed in the stock exchange (i.e. that are registered with the CVM); (2) banks and financial institutions; (3) transnational companies with subsidiaries in Brazil; or (4) other non-listed companies, including private limited partnerships.

Both listed and unlisted business entities are subject to the requirements of the Corporate Act. Listed companies are required to follow CVM-approved accounting standards. They also are required to have their financial statements audited by independent auditors. In general, unlisted companies usually apply accounting standards established by the CVM.

Banks and financial institutions are required to follow accounting standards set by the National Monetary Council and the Central Bank of Brazil. There are more than 2,450 institutions supervised by the Central Bank of Brazil,[4] with the top ten banks making up more than 65 per cent of the total assets of the national financial system. These entities follow a prescribed chart of accounts (known as the accounting plan for institutions of the national financial system). Banks and financial institutions are to follow recognition, measurement and disclosure criteria consistent with IFRS.

---

[4] More information is available at www.bcb.gov.br.

Transnational corporations or subsidiaries of foreign companies in, among others, the automobile, chemical, pharmaceutical, paper and cardboard and foodstuffs industries are usually established as limited liability partnerships and are not required to provide financial statements. They are not subject to audits by independent auditors. Where audit reports are prepared, they are meant for use in managerial decision-making.

Other companies not included in the previous categories are not required to report and disclose their financial statements or be audited by independent auditors. They are required to provide some company information only to the Federal Tax Revenue Service in accordance with tax law.

As mentioned previously, Brazilian accounting has been traditionally subject to legislation and regulation by government bodies. Progress in developing accounting principles and concepts has not been fast. It was only in 1972 that the Federal Accountancy Council (CFC), (resolution 321/72) and the Central Bank of Brazil (instruction 179/72) included the wording "accounting principles" as part of the requirements for financial reporting by listed companies. There was no definition of these accounting principles, however.

In accordance with the requirements of the Institute of Independent Auditors of Brazil (IBRACON), the auditor's report had to state whether the financial statements were in conformity with generally accepted accounting principles or not. However, IBRACON did not provide details on such principles either.

It was not until 1981 that the CFC issued a resolution which defined what was applicable in Brazil. However, this did not affect the basic accounting principles (as opposed to generally accepted accounting principles and auditors in practical terms), as the prevailing thinking was that it was more important to ensure that financial statements were in accordance with legislation or regulatory requirements than with accounting principles.

Further steps were taken in 1993, when the CFC published another resolution (replacing the 1981 resolution) defining seven basic accounting principles, namely: legal entity, going-concern, historical cost, prudence, accrual basis, objectivity and monetary adjustment. In 1996, the CFC established a working group, composed of accounting experts, to developing accounting standards for Brazil. This working group comprised of members of various Brazilian regulatory agencies, such as the CVM, the Central Bank, the Superintendence of Private Insurance, the Federal Revenue Service, the National Treasury Secretariat and the Brazilian Institute of Independent Auditors.

One of the main objectives of the working group was to propose ways of adapting Brazilian accounting practices to standards issued by the International Accounting Standards Committee (the predecessor of the IASB). Accounting standards issued by the CFC do not have legal authority since the CFC is not recognized in Brazilian law as an accounting standard-setter for regulatory filing purposes. Only accounting standards issued by the CFC and approved by the CVM become mandatory for listed companies. However, the CFC could sanction its members for not following its accounting standards in preparing general-purpose financial statements.

Significant changes have also taken place in the area of audit regulation in Brazil. Auditing gained more importance in the 1970s after listed companies were required to have their financial statements audited by independent auditors. Previously, audited financial statements had been required only for subsidiaries of transnational corporations, or as part of requirements for submitting loan applications to private or public financial institutions.

At present, in addition to listed companies, other public service companies regulated by the Federal Government, for example, banks, insurance companies, telephone service providers and utility companies, are required to have their financial statements audited by independent auditors. Currently, the Brazilian Securities Commission requires that new accountants who apply for accreditation as independent auditors must pass a technical examination. As of May 2006, 481 firms were officially recognized as independent auditors in Brazil.[5]

The CVM and the Central Bank of Brazil require independent auditors to be rotated every five years. After rotation, independent auditors could be hired once again by the same client after a break of three years. This requirement is intended to avoid auditors losing their impartiality if they maintained a long-term relationship with a client.

In accordance with current regulation, audit firms in Brazil have the option of participating in peer-review programmes. Independent audit firms apply auditing standards which are very similar to the ones issued by the American Institute of Certified Public Accountants or the International Auditing and Assurance Standards Board of IFAC. Furthermore, in accordance with emerging international good practice, independent audit firms in Brazil are prohibited from providing consulting services to their audit clients. They are, however, allowed to provide advice on tax planning and other similar activities which, in Brazil, are considered to be compatible with the duties of an independent auditor.

Education and business culture are, in general, important factors affecting the pace of convergence of Brazilian accounting standards and IFRS. The quality of accounting education and the status of the accounting profession in a given country has had a significant impact on the quality of financial information that an accounting system is required and able to produce. Significant efforts have been undertaken in the country over recent years to improve the quality of accounting education.

The first accounting school in Brazil, the Alvares Penteado Foundation, was established in Sao Paulo in 1906. It was strongly influenced by the Italian school of accountancy that emphasized the double-entry bookkeeping system rather than reporting concepts. This style of accounting education prevailed until the mid-1970s before financial reforms took place and the Corporate Act was introduced.

At present, 885 university accounting programmes authorized by the Ministry of Education are being delivered throughout Brazil. Most of the institutions that deliver accounting education are located in the Southern and South-Eastern regions of the country. In 2005, about 150,000 accounting students were enrolled in these institutions. It is important to note that the University of Sao Paulo was the first educational institution in Brazil that was authorized to regularly accept students for graduate and doctoral degree programmes. As of 30 April 2006, the university had conferred a total of 147 doctorates in accounting.

Accounting as a profession in Brazil is still not as well-known or held in such wide regard as it is in some other countries with a long history of accounting. In general, the prevailing opinion is that accountants are responsible for bookkeeping and corporate tax. Accounting education at master's and PhD level attracts less than 1 per cent of all undergraduate students in accounting. Research on international accounting in the form of dissertations, theses and publications in professional and academic journals is still not significant. As a result, expertise on international accounting matters is highly concentrated in a small number of experts and professional accountants. One of main obstacles is the fact that these standards are written in

---

[5] More information is available at www.cvm.gov.br.

English and are not widely available in languages that most professional accountants in Brazil could easily understand.

In Brazil, there are two bodies that are designated to regulate and supervise the accounting profession. These are the CFC and IBRACON. The CFC is a representative agency of the Brazilian accounting profession created by Decree No. 9295/46 to supervise professional accounting practice in Brazil.

Prior to 1999, all persons who held a bachelor degree in accounting and who graduated from an academic institution accredited by the Ministry of the Education were eligible to practice accounting by registering with a regional accountancy council. In 1999, a new regulation that required candidates to pass a qualifying examination was introduced. The pass rate fluctuated between 50 per cent and 65 per cent of the total number of candidates enrolled.

According to the CFC, 393,382 accountants are currently licensed to practice as independent auditors. Of these, 200,707, or 51 per cent, are accounting technicians or secondary school graduates and 192,875, or 49 per cent, hold bachelor degrees in accounting.

Furthermore, the CFC established requirements for continuing professional development for independent auditors. Accordingly, independent auditors were required to undertake 24 hours of continuing professional development during 2003 and 32 hours annually after that. Activities that qualify for continuing professional development were specified in CFC resolution 945/02. The continuing professional development requirements are expected to apply to all accountants licensed by the CFC.

Comparison of Brazilian accounting standards with IFRS

According to research by the CVM,[6] the convergence process of Brazilian standards and IFRS is developing at a moderate pace.

Recently, the CVM[7] presented the main differences between Brazilian accounting standards and IFRS. The following deserve special mention: (1) the introduction and application of the fair value measurements, particularly by non-financial companies; (2) accounting for financial instruments in relation to fair value; (3) accounting for and reporting on finance leases in financial statements; (4) business combinations; (5) accounting for government grants; and (6) segment reporting.

The following is a brief description of some of accounting requirements in Brazil, principally those that differ from IFRS.

Inventory

Inventory measurement criteria in Brazilian legislation are similar to those of the IASB. The first-in-first-out, weighted average and lower of cost or net realizable value are accepted methods of valuation. Interest related to the acquisition of inventory is treated as an expense, in the manner required in IAS 2 on inventories.

Construction contracts

Long-term construction contracts, especially civil construction contracts, are subject to fiscal rules that affect the general-purpose financial statement of construction companies. Tax

---

[6] Official Memorandum/CVM/SNC/SEP No. 01/2006.
[7] *Ibid.*

regulations require that revenue from construction contracts be recognized on a cash basis. It is important to remember that most companies active in the construction industry are limited liability companies that are not required to publish their financial statements. The small number of publicly traded corporations is subject to CVM standards that require recognition of revenue based on the percentage-of-completion method.

Joint ventures and consolidation

In Brazil, legally established joint ventures are treated in the same way as other corporate interests and consolidated using either the cost or equity method. Consolidation is mandatory only for companies regulated by the CVM and the Corporate Act.

Impairment

Brazilian standards require that recoverable value be based on the present value of future cash flows, regardless of the net selling price.

At present impairment testing is required only for listed companies, and only with respect to specific assets such as property, plant and equipment.

Property, plant and equipment – revaluation and subsequent costs

Revaluation

Brazilian standards require that property, plant and equipment should be valued using the cost model, i.e., the historical cost less any accumulated depreciation. The revaluation model is an allowed alternative; however, it is not applied routinely. The general tendency in Brazil has been to apply revalue property, plant and equipment in limited circumstances, for example, when mergers, incorporation and other corporate restructuring occur.

Some discrepancies in accounting practices regarding procedures for tax deferral and downward revaluation exist, but are not significant. It is important to remember that, in previous years, revaluation of assets was inappropriately used in Brazil as a way of increasing assets and equity. Currently, recognizing inflationary effects on financial statements is prohibited under corporate reporting law and tax regulation.

Subsequent costs

Some differences between Brazilian accounting standards and IFRS can been seen in how they account for subsequent costs incurred in relation to property, plant and equipment. According to IFRS, these costs should be expensed when incurred, unless these expenses contribute towards increasing the future economic benefits of the related item of property, plant and equipment. In Brazil, subsequent costs that cannot be capitalized as items of property, plant and equipment are recorded as deferred expenses and must be amortized over a period of 10 years in accordance with corporate law or within five years according to tax legislation.

Research and development costs

Accounting for research and development expenses constitutes one of main areas where there is discrepancy between Brazilian standards and IFRS. According to IFRS, costs incurred during the phase of researching new products should be recorded as expenses. Costs incurred during the development phase can be capitalized only when certain specific conditions stipulated by the IASB are met, namely: technical feasibility of completing the intangible asset so that it will be available for use or sale; viability of use or sale; probability of generating future economic benefits; availability of adequate technical, financial and other resources to complete the development and use or sell the intangible asset; and ability to measure reliably the expenditure attributable to the intangible asset during its development. In Brazil, research and development costs must be capitalized and amortized over a period of 10 years; however, recent accounting practice in Brazil has favoured expensing all research and development costs, in accordance with tax legislation, on the grounds of uncertainty in obtaining future benefits from the products for which the costs were incurred.

Intangible assets (other than goodwill)

In accordance with IFRS, expenses incurred for software development for internal use are expensed when incurred; however, Brazilian standards allow entities to defer expensing costs incurred for the development of new software systems.

Revenue recognition

Generally speaking, there are no significant differences between Brazilian and international standards on the recognition of revenue.

Financial instruments

With regard to accounting and reporting on financial instruments in Brazil, a distinction has to be made between financial and non-financial institutions, as the former are subject to mandatory accounting procedures issued by the Central Bank of Brazil. The recognition and measurement requirements that banks and financial institutions need to adhere to are essentially those stipulated in IFRS, including with respect to classification as mark-to-market and hedging; however, the extent of disclosure required in Brazil is lower than that required in IFRS.

In contrast, Brazilian corporate legislation makes no provision regarding financial instruments. As a result, listed companies apply CVM requirements. In general, these corporations treat certain financial instruments as off-balance-sheet items. The CVM only requires disclosure of estimated market value of financial instruments in the notes to the financial statements. Some of the alternative valuations that are allowed include the value that could be obtained by trading a similar financial instrument, or the adjusted present value based on current market interest rates for similar financial instruments. In this respect, the notes become more important than the financial statements.

Accounting policies, changes in accounting estimates and errors

IFRS require corrections of errors to be made by re-stating comparative amounts from a prior period; if the error occurred prior to the earliest period presented in the financial statements, this needs to be re-stated in the opening balance sheet. The common practice in Brazil is re-stating the opening balance sheet. Although convergence in this area is not perfect, users are not disadvantaged as long as the procedures applied are clearly stated in the notes to the financial statements.

Leasing

Finance leases represent one of the difficult accounting problems in Brazil, particularly with respect to achieving convergence between Brazilian standards and IFRS. According to Brazilian tax regulations, all leases are accounted for using procedures similar to operating leases. Thus, lease transactions that are predominantly financial in nature are accounted for in a manner similar to operating leases. The lessee is not required to reflect the value of the leased asset and the corresponding liability in the balance sheet. It is worth noting that the CFC has published accounting requirements for leases similar to IFRS, but, like above-mentioned CFC standards, they are not mandatory.

With regard to leaseback operations, IFRS stipulates different approaches depending on the circumstances of the transaction. If the transaction results in a finance lease, any profit should be deferred and amortized over the lease term. If it results in an operating lease, the profit or loss should be recognized immediately. In Brazil, profit obtained by the lessee on the sale of the leased asset must be recognized at the time of the transaction. Tax regulations prohibit deferral of such profit.

Government grants

Under Brazilian accounting standards, government investment grants are recognized in a capital reserve in equity when received and without any specific link to the assets or the project's lifespan. IFRS require that they should be recognized only when there is a reasonable certainty concerning compliance with conditions for receiving the grant.

Effects of changes in foreign exchange rates

In general, conversion and consolidation procedures in Brazil requiring the use of exchange rates are essentially those required by IFRS. This reasonable degree of convergence with IFRS could possibly be explained by the influence of independent auditors in large accounting firms who work both in Brazil and abroad.

Business combinations

In Brazil, there is no legal obligation to assess the fair value of assets and liabilities when a business combination takes place. It is usually done for management purposes, to determine the value of the asset which is being restructured. By contrast, this is mandatory in IFRS.

With respect to premiums and discounts in acquisitions of investments assessed by the equity method, amortization of goodwill deriving from expected future results cannot exceed 10 years (according to the CVM), while IFRS stipulates that goodwill should not be amortized but tested for impairment annually.

With respect to business combinations in Brazil, the legal form is more important than the essence of the transaction. IFRS principally require an assessment of the essence of the deal and consider practically all business combination transactions as acquisitions, unless it is impossible to identify the buyer. In comparing CVM standards with IASB goodwill requirements (on business combinations), the following specific procedures are worth mentioning:

(a)   Goodwill is recorded according to its economic basis under CVM standards, whereas under IFRS it is recorded as goodwill resulting from a business acquisition;

(b)   IFRS obliges the acquirer to recognize in profit and loss the acquirer's interest in the net fair value of the acquired asset that exceeds the cost of the combination. However, in accordance with CVM standards in force in Brazil, this is taken into account to reduce the equity of the investment to which it refers.

Investments in associates

In order to apply the equity method to investments in associated companies, Brazilian accounting standards require ownership of 20 per cent or more of the associated company's capital. IFRS stipulate that if an investor, directly or indirectly, holds 20 per cent or more of the voting power of the investee, it is presumed that the investor has significant influence and the equity method must be used.

The CVM standard is similar to that of the IASB, in that it stipulates that investments in subsidiaries do not necessarily have to be significant in order to apply the equity method; however, they differ in that CVM standards stipulate that the equity method can be applied for all associated companies with a minimum of a 10 per cent investment in the company's capital, while the IASB determines that it can only be applied when there is a minimum of 20 per cent ownership of voting stock.

Finally, there are some technical differences in the calculation and determination of equity related to provisions, reporting dates, etc..

Employee benefits

Listed companies in Brazil recognize and measure employee benefits in accordance with an IBRACON-issued standard. The CVM subsequently made the IBRACON standard mandatory for listed companies. The objective of IFRS and Brazilian accounting standards on employee benefits is to establish the accounting and disclosure requirement for employee benefits, including short-term benefits, pensions, post-employment life insurance and medical benefits and other long-term employment benefits. The Brazilian standard deals with benefits to which employees will be entitled after their time of service, whether paid directly to employees or indirectly through contributions to a social security entity.

Certain companies use cash-based accounting, while others do not have to use it at all, as they do not have employee-benefit programmes because the Federal Government has an official retirement plan to which both employer and employee contribute.

Interest payments on shareholders' equity

In Brazil, interest payments related to remuneration on shareholders' equity are treated as an expense by tax legislation and as a reduction of the earned surplus account by corporate legislation. Under both types of legislation, this interest essentially represents dividend payments. IFRS require that dividend payments on shares that are wholly recognized as liabilities should be treated in the same way as interest payments on bonds.

Cash flow statement

Cash flow statements are optional in Brazil, but supplementary information is required by IFRS. The statement of source and application of funds (known in Portuguese under the acronym DOAR) is a requirement. Replacing the DOAR with a cash flow statement is one of the goals of convergence with IFRS. This has been proposed as one of the amendments to the country's Corporation Act.

Earnings per share

In Brazil, earnings per share are calculated by dividing fiscal-year net profit by the number of common and preferred stocks in circulation at the end of the period, while IFRS require calculation by dividing the period's net profit or loss attributable to common stockholders by the weighted average of the number of common stock outstanding during the period. Unlike under IFRS, calculation of diluted earnings per share is not required in Brazil.

Segment reporting

Brazilian accounting standards do not require information or reports on business segments. The CVM has published a voluntary orientation report recommending that listed companies provide segment-level reporting.

Interim financial statements

In Brazil, only financial institutions – as required under the legislation of the Central Bank of Brazil – are obliged to prepare and publish monthly and half-yearly balance sheets. Listed companies must prepare quarterly information to be made available to the stock exchange and investors.

Provisions, contingent liabilities and contingent assets

Brazilian and IFRS requirements are similar with respect to recognition of contingencies.

III. Lessons learned

The need to improve the efficiency of the development of accounting standards is recognized in Brazil. Various efforts are being undertaken to improve the standard-setting process. These efforts are expected to result in: (1) harmonization of accounting standards for different business sectors; (2) greater alignment with international standards; and (3) faster turnaround time for implementing new standards.

One of the main lessons learned so far during the process of convergence of Brazilian accounting standards and IFRS was the need for better coordination of efforts among the various organizations involved in this process. As a number of agencies are involved in the regulatory processes affecting accounting, legislative approval of proposed accounting standards calls for extensive consultations and takes a considerable amount of time. As a result, accounting standards are not keeping pace with changes in the business environment.

Therefore, in recent years, there has been increased interaction between the CVM and IBRACON with a view to harmonizing the standards issued by the two agencies. IBRACON has worked jointly with the CVM and its consultative body on accounting standards, with a view to gradually reducing the current differences between Brazilian accounting standards and IFRS.

Another important development in Brazil is a bill (No. 3741/2000) that is currently being considered by the Finances and Tax Commission of the Brazilian Congress's Chamber of Deputies. It proposes various measures to promote convergence between Brazilian standards and IFRS that are expected to facilitate the process.

The main proposals of the bill include: creating a single entity responsible for preparing and issuing accounting standards; ensuring CVM-issued standards conform with IFRS; clearly separating tax legislation from financial reporting requirements; making cash flow statements mandatory for listed companies; making the presentation of the economic value added obligatory; and requiring that large companies, corporations, private companies and limited liability companies disclose their audited financial statements.

As discussed above, IFRS expertise in Brazil is currently highly concentrated in a small circle of professional accountants. Therefore, further concerted efforts are needed in the area of education and training on IFRS-related issues.

There is a strong need for greater international cooperation to ensure a wider dissemination of knowledge on IFRS, including in languages that are easily understood in Brazil. The IASB could facilitate access to IFRS by conducting a series of technical discussions in Brazil, thus enhancing communication and expertise.

IV. Conclusions

The Brazilian legal culture has heavily influenced on the country's system of accounting. Act No. 6404/76 has defined in detail the accounting standards that corporations must follow. The Corporate Act contains accounting standards that in other countries are developed by a whole series of rules and regulations. Therefore, to change an accounting standard prescribed by the law, another law must be passed, which causes the process of change in the Brazilian system of accounting to be slow and inflexible.

Despite this challenge, modern accounting in Brazil has evolved through legally constituted agencies that supervise and inspect the financial market. However, this evolution has been slowed by lack of coordination between related regulatory bodies, in particular, between the CVM (which supervises and inspects the capital market for non-financial institutions) and the Central Bank of Brazil's Department of Banking Standards and Inspection (which monitors financial institutions).

The new Corporate Act, contained in bill No. 3741/2000 and on which consultations have been conducted in the Congress for over five years, proposes substantive changes in the formal structure used for developing the country's accounting standards. The law is expected to abandon the current scope of prescriptive accounting rules and will instead take on an authorizing role. The process of developing standards will then be conducted by an independent agency that will be established by the law, comprising professionals with specific expertise and academics, trade associations, and businesses. It is hoped that this change will increase quality, speed and convergence with IFRS.

Chapter III

Case study of Germany

I. Introduction[1]

Germany has a long tradition of accounting regulation, which has always been the responsibility of the legislator.[2] Many changes have taken place in recent years in the accounting environment as a result of European regulations and numerous national laws, and changes in capital markets. Predominant triggers for change were the increasing importance of capital markets in providing financing and the internationalization of investors. Consequently, new demands on accounting arose, especially with regard to timely and decision-useful investor information.

The question is how traditional German generally accepted accounting principles (GAAP) will adapt to or coexist with international accounting systems, whose influence is constantly increasing. In addition to accounting regulation, new enforcement regulations were developed to enhance both investor protection and market efficiency. Financial scandals such as Enron, WorldCom or Parmalat scandals have brought to the fore the need for revised enforcement regulations worldwide. Furthermore, the European Union requirement for all listed companies to prepare their consolidated financial statements in accordance with international financial reporting standards (IFRS)[3] demands effective enforcement.

This study illustrates the process of implementing IFRS in Germany. It begins by explaining the structure of traditional German GAAP in order to point out the fundamental conflicts accompanying the implementation of IFRS (sect. II). Owing to market forces, German GAAP opened up, and internationally accepted accounting standards were integrated in the German legal system. Section III describes exactly how capacity was built and what institutional structures were needed to integrate and efficiently allow for the application of such a fundamentally different accounting system. In section IV, specific transition issues and the predominant technical issue with regard to IFRS are outlined. The study concludes by summarizing the results and presenting the outlook for the future.

---

[1] This chapter was prepared and edited by the UNCTAD secretariat with substantive inputs from Kati Beierdorf and Kristina Schwedler of the Accounting Standards Committee of Germany.

[2] The first uniform accounting law (General German Commercial Code), which was adopted as early as 1861, requires all entities – independent of legal form or size – to prepare financial statements.

[3] For the purpose of this chapter, IFRS also comprise International Accounting Standards (IAS) and related interpretations (Standing Interpretations Committee and International Financial Reporting Interpretations Committee (IFRIC) interpretations).

II. German financial reporting system and the need for internationally accepted accounting standards

German accounting system

Main features of the German Commercial Code

German GAAP are principle-based accounting standards. They consist of underlying principles, known as principles of proper bookkeeping, which are both codified and non-codified. The source for the codified principles of proper bookkeeping and the majority of further accounting standards is the German Commercial Code. Legal requirements often lack detailed descriptions of specific accounting issues, for example, guidance on leasing accounting; therefore, additional literature and court decisions interpreting accounting issues are an essential part of the accounting system. The German GAAP thus evolved over time and adjusted gradually to the changes in the accounting environment.

Each accounting system needs to define its objectives and develop accounting standards accordingly; for example, financial statements according to German GAAP are not only prepared to provide information for investors,[1] but also function as the basis for determining distributable profits which serve to protect creditors of the company. Creditor protection is the predominant objective in Germany and, as a result, German GAAP focus on capital maintenance, as creditors are mainly interested in the capital remaining in the company to build up and strengthen the capacity to repay debt when due.

However, only the separate financial statements[2] serve as a basis for determining distributable profits. In addition, separate financial statements serve as a basis for tax accounting. The initial idea of implementing the conformity principle[3] was to simplify accounting. Companies were to prepare only one balance sheet serving commercial and tax purposes. However, tax accounting did not use only commercial accounting regulations. Over time, additional tax regulations were adopted. In order to continue to prepare one single balance sheet, some tax accounting standards are accepted under Commercial Code. For example, article 254 of the Commercial Code states that additional depreciations are acceptable in order to carry items of fixed or current assets at the lower value that results from the application of accelerated tax depreciation. In addition, accounting options under the code are carried out in accordance with the tax requirements. Therefore, tax regulation influences financial statements under the code. Contrary to the various objectives of separate financial statements (such as profit distribution, basis for tax accounting and information for general users) consolidated financial statements are prepared solely for information purposes.

Since capital maintenance is generally sought by creditors, German GAAP comprise numerous principles which together form a prudent accounting system. An important feature of

---

[1] While the current IASB Framework acknowledges many different users of financial statements, IFRS focus on the investors. It is assumed that other users' needs are satisfied by providing information according to investors' needs.

[2] In this chapter, separate financial statements refer to the individual accounts of legal entities (non-consolidated).

[3] The conformity principle states that the separate financial statements are used for tax purposes, unless specific tax regulations require a departure from German GAAP.

this accounting system is the imparity principle, which can be divided into the realization principle and the anticipation-of-loss principle. The realization principle ensures that only realized gains are recognized as profits; the anticipation-of-loss principle requires accounting for unrealized losses. For example, property (cost = € 1 million), whose value increased over time (fair value = € 2 million) is still measured at cost in the balance sheet. If the value decreases (fair value = € 0.5 million) the property is impaired and has to be written down in the balance sheet to the lower value, with the impairment loss recognized in profit and loss. As a result, increases and decreases in value are treated differently, as German GAAP follow a strict lower-of-cost or market principle. Further examples of the importance of prudence are non-recognition of internally generated intangible fixed assets (see art. 248 (2) of the code) and no revenue recognition according to the percentage of completion method.[4] The same principles and accounting regulations apply to consolidated financial statements, even though they only serve for information purposes.

German Commercial Code in the light of European accounting regulations

The objective of the European Union (EU) has always been to harmonize legal requirements in its member States in order to create a more efficient European market.[5] To achieve a more transparent and hence more efficient capital market, the need for harmonized accounting regulations was acknowledged. The EU published the fourth (on annual accounts) and seventh (on consolidated accounts) Council directives,[6] providing for legal measures which each Member State is required to enact in national law. The directives did not succeed in fully harmonizing accounting requirements throughout the EU, as the directives included numerous member State options and were given different national interpretations. As a result, the directives did not meet the needs of companies that wished to raise capital on pan-European or international securities markets.[7]

In 2000, the EU chose a different legal measure, i.e., a regulation as opposed to a Directive. It concluded that the vision of a single European financial market based on transparent and comparable financial statements called for unambiguous accounting standards. While the European Commission had expressed its preference for IFRS as the set of standards for listed European companies as early as 1995,[8] it was not until 2000 that the European Commission announced its intention to require the application of IFRS for consolidated financial statements from 2005 onwards. A regulation on the application of international accounting standards[9] was finally adopted in 2002. The mandatory application of IFRS for listed companies preparing consolidated accounts entered directly into force in all member States under the IAS

---

[4] Instead, the completed contract method is used.

[5] The first treaty creating the European Community was signed on 18 April 1951. The Treaty on the European Union was signed in Maastricht on 7 February 1992.

[6] Fourth Council Directive of 25 July 1978 (78/660/EEC). *Official Journal (OJ) of the European Community J L 222.* 14 August 1978: 11; Seventh Council Directive of 13 June 1983 (83/349/EEC). *OJ L 193.* 18 July 1983: 1. See p.2 of the Fourth Directive for details about reasons. The directives were implemented in Germany in 1985. With the implementation of these directives, previously fragmented German accounting laws were restructured to form a broad accounting regulation for all companies (Third Edition of German Commercial Code).

[7] The EU has also come to this conclusion been. See, for example, European Commission COM (2000) 359, 13 June 2000 and, for more details on the options: Roques. *Service Statistics and the International Harmonization of Accounting Rules.* 1996: 284 seq.

[8] See European Commission, COM (1995) 508, 14.11.1995 "Accounting Harmonization: A new strategy vis-à-vis international harmonization".

[9] See Regulation (EC) No. 1606/2002 of the European Parliament and of the Council of 19 July 2002. *OJ L 243.* 11 September 2002: 1. IAS Regulation.

Regulation.[10] Member State options were solely granted with regard to the requirement or permission of IFRS for non-listed companies preparing consolidated accounts and/or for companies preparing annual statutory accounts. Without member State options or possible delayed implementation, the foundations for uniform and comparable financial statements on the European capital market were established.

Enforcement of German GAAP

The German Commercial Code requires the annual financial statements and management report of corporations to be audited by auditors,[11] who secure the proper application of the accounting standards. Furthermore, to ensure conformity with the applicable accounting standards, penalties (imprisonment of up to three years or a monetary fine) are imposed if accounting standards are violated.[12] In addition to the audit requirements of the German Commercial Code, the Certified Auditors (Regulation of the Profession) Act[13] (which addresses admission requirements and the rights and duties of a certified auditor) must be observed.

All legal requirements are reviewed and updated on a regular basis. For example, in 1998, civil penalty provisions were tightened (art. 334 of the code) and a mandatory auditor rotation system was introduced (art. 319a (1) No. 4 of the code), while in 2001 peer reviews (an external quality control) by other auditors were introduced.

The Chamber of Public Accountants and the Institute of Public Accountants in Germany are the authoritative institutions in ensuring the efficiency of audits of financial reporting instruments. The Chamber of Public Accountants is a public body, under public supervision, in which public accountants/auditors and accounting firms are organized on a mandatory basis. Its tasks are codified and include quality control of its members or conduction of aptitude tests.[14]

The Institute of Public Accountants, on the other hand, is a private-sector association in which public auditors and auditing companies are organized on a voluntary basis. Technical issues of the profession are analysed and GAAP are usually developed by this institution. Through its auditing standards and auditing guidelines, the institute makes a significantly contribution to high-quality standardized auditing of financial reports in Germany.

The need for internationally accepted standards: pioneers

In the course of globalization of business activities, large German companies had an increased demand for capital and were eager to participate in large international capital markets, especially the New York Stock Exchange – the largest capital market in the world.

However, financial reports prepared according to German GAAP were not accepted on this market. At first, the problem of acceptance arose mainly because German GAAP was not known outside of Germany. In due course, companies were obliged to prepare additional financial statements in accordance with United States GAAP in order to be listed on the New York Stock Exchange.

DaimlerChrysler AG (formerly listed as Daimler Benz AG) was a pioneer in this area, preparing additional consolidated annual financial statements to meet United States GAAP. In

---

[10] See art. 4 of the IAS Regulation.

[11] In 1931, the obligation to audit annual financial statements was adopted in the German Commercial Code (art. 316 of the Code).

[12] See art. 331 of the code.

[13] Gesetz über eine Berufsordnung der Wirtschaftsprüfer (Wirtschaftsprüferordnung).

[14] For further information, see www.wpk.de/english/ and www.idw.de.

1996, many other companies, such as Deutsche Telekom, Fresenius Medical Care AG, Pfeiffer Vacuum Technology AG, followed DaimlerChrysler to the New York Stock Exchange; Digitale Telekabel AG, for example, was listed on the NASDAQ stock market.[15]

Yet, companies were not solely driven by access to new sources of finances. Several other reasons drove them to seek a listing on the New York Stock Exchange, including:

- Listing as a marketing instrument (no other listing involves such publicity and makes the company known worldwide);
- Improving company image and presentation to investors;
- Aligning external financial reporting and internal management accounting to allow for a more efficient internal planning and control;[16]
- Preparing for buy-outs abroad, if shares are to be used as acquisition currency.

In 1994, the first dual consolidated financial statements were prepared by companies in the pharmaceutical and chemical industry, such as Schering AG. A dual financial report is prepared under the German Commercial Code using all accounting choices that were available in IAS. [17] At that time, IAS tended to be closer to German GAAP and, compared to United States GAAP, IAS provided more accounting options. In addition, German GAAP group accounts were still required when preparing the necessary dual group accounts and, as a result, it appeared to be less burdensome to follow IAS than United States GAAP.

Later other companies were listed on the New Stock Exchange in Germany, which had been established in 1997 to give smaller growth companies the opportunity to raise equity. One of the prerequisites for accessing this market segment was to prepare financial statements in accordance with internationally accepted accounting standards (IFRS or United States GAAP).

The extent to which the international accounting systems differed from national GAAP became obvious when financial statements were prepared in accordance with national GAAP and the figures were compared with those prepared under IFRS or United States GAAP. Substantial discrepancies in the given information and specific accounting positions were revealed. DaimlerChrysler, for example, had an increase in equity of 8 billion Deutsche Marks (= € 4.1 billion) and a resulting profit decrease of 2.5 billion Deutsche Marks (= € 1.3 billion). The main differences and effects will be presented in section III of this study.

Consequently, German GAAP did not enjoy positive publicity. From an international accounting perspective (the point of view of capital market investors), German GAAP are not popular, partly because of its following features:

- Overemphasis on creditors and thus too much emphasis on the prudence principle;
- Artificial stabilization of profits by building-up and reducing hidden reserves, thereby making it difficult to identify a company crisis and then perhaps only with a time lag (until hidden reserves have been used up);
- Tax accounting affecting commercial accounting and distorting the objectives of the commercial balance sheet;

---

[15] Seventeen German companies are currently listed on the NYSE and two on the NASDAQ.

[16] In Germany, external financial reporting and internal management accounting are completely separate systems. Because of the focus of external financial reporting on creditor protection, it is of little use for internal management purposes.

[17] Any remaining differences were usually immaterial, thereby allowing the financial statements to be labelled IFRS financial statements.

- Major recognition and measurement issues not explicitly addressed in the German Commercial Code;
- Too many accounting policy choices (e.g. in relation to goodwill or measurement of inventories);
- Distortion of results of operations (e.g. provisions for certain expenses permitted).

III. Integration of international financial reporting standards into the German financial reporting system

Regulatory framework

Towards international financial reporting standards

The German legislator (Parliament) realized that both previous EU efforts to harmonize accounting regulation and existing German GAAP did not live up to the expectations and demands of German capital market-oriented companies. Germany responded accordingly by opening up its accounting system to internationally accepted accounting standards long before any EU legal measure on the application of IFRS was decided upon. In 1998, the national legislator allowed listed companies[18] to prepare consolidated financial statements in accordance with internationally accepted accounting standards (IFRS or United States GAAP) instead of German GAAP.[19] As already mentioned, consolidated financial statements – contrary to separate financial statements – are prepared solely for information purposes, so this concession did not seem to interfere with other national accounting issues.[20]

The legislator – expecting developments in the EU – viewed this concession as an interim solution, effective only until 31 December 2004, and German requirements regarding consolidated accounts were to be brought in line with international requirements before that date. To support the legislator in this ambitious task, a privately organized institution was established in 1998, the Accounting Standards Committee of Germany (ASCG), and its standard setting body, the German Accounting Standards Board (GASB). The ASCG is authorized by article 342 of the Commercial Code to:

- Develop recommendations on the application of German accepted group accounting principles (German accounting standards);
- Advise the Federal Ministry of Justice on accounting regulations; and
- Represent Germany in international standard-setting bodies.

For the first time, a private institution was assigned by the legislator to address accounting issues. There were several reservations, especially as to independence and credibility of a privately organized accounting standard setting body and the legal effect of standards developed by this institution; however, a private accounting standards body allowed greater flexibility in the

---

[18] These initially only included companies which were issuing equity. Later, all capital market-oriented companies were included (issuers of equity and issuers of debt).

[19] The legislator temporarily (until 31 December 2004) adopted art. 292a of the German Commercial Code.

[20] Accounting experts predicted impacts on separate financial accounts, however, since legal requirements concerning consolidated accounts refer to recognition and measurement requirements for separate accounts. See art. 298 (1) of the Commercial Code.

development of accounting and financial reporting principles and a quick adaptation of such principles to meet the changing needs of preparers and users of financial statements. Furthermore, the due process allowed all parties interested in accounting issues to be included.

The ASCG is organized similarly to the International Accounting Standards Committee (IASC) Foundation. The GASB comprises independent accounting experts with different backgrounds, including academics, preparers (industrial and financial businesses), analysts and auditors. To complete the structure of the GASC, the Accounting Interpretations Committee was founded in 2004. The Committee handles on national issues relate to the application of IFRS. It subsequently analyses whether this is a solely national or internationally relevant issue. Depending on its conclusion, it will refer the issue to the relevant international organization (i.e. IFRIC) or develop a specific national guideline for the application of the IFRS in question. Figure 1 gives an overview of the structure of the ASCG.

Figure 1. Overview of the structure of the ASCG

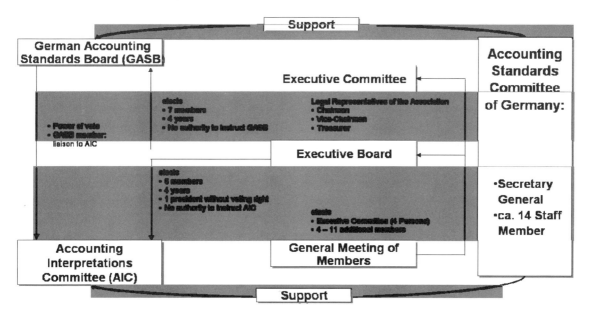

To date, the German accounting standards have had a great impact on the preparation of financial reports under the Commercial Code. In particular, the standards fill gaps in legal requirements, e.g. on management reports, risk reports, cash flow statements, segment reporting or statement of changes in equity, and have changed and harmonized the national financial reporting tremendously. However, there are still doubts as to the degree of legal authority of these standards. This is due partly to preparers and auditors questioning the legal authority of German accounting standards and partly to lack of enforcement. In particular, standards which limit accounting choices existing under the Commercial Code are rarely being applied (e.g. GAS 4 on acquisition accounting in consolidated financial statements).

At the same time, the Commercial Code has undergone further developments. For example, article 297 of the code expanded requirements with regard to the elements of consolidated financial reporting by cash flow statements and statement of changes in equity.

Current situation: Coexistence of IFRS and German GAAP

With the adoption of the IAS Regulation, the Commercial Code's authorization of IFRS or United States GAAP consolidated accounts became obsolete and was replaced by the requirement for listed companies to prepare consolidated accounts in accordance with IFRS. As mentioned above, EU member States had the option of allowing or requiring IFRS for other companies as well. Because of the objectives of separate financial statements (see sect. II), which IFRS accounts supposedly were not adequately designed to fulfil, Germany has chosen a less rigorous approach on the implementation of the options, which is shown in the figure below:

Figure 2. German GAAP and IFRS

	Group Accounts	Individual Accounts
LISTED Companies	**IFRS MANDATORY since 2005** Obligation Effective from 2007 for Listed debt instruments and users of US GAAP	IFRS: Prohibited ⇨ German GAAP Accounts Still Mandatory
NON-LISTED Companies	IFRS: Option	Large Companies may file IFRS financial statements with the Federal Gazette IFRS: Prohibited ⇨ German GAAP Accounts Still Mandatory

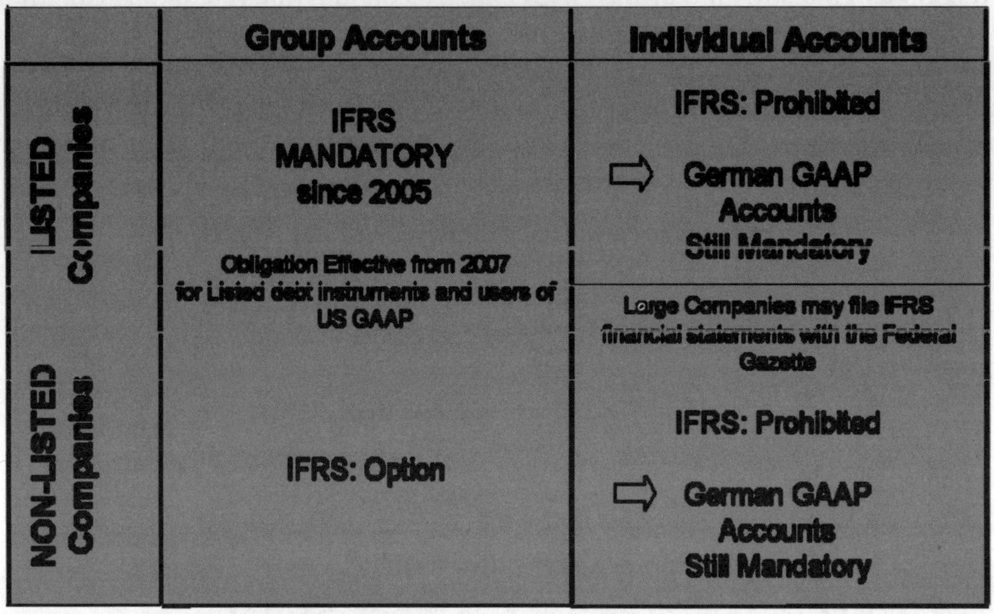

As shown in figure 2, German GAAP and IFRS (until 2007, this was also true of United States GAAP) currently co-exist when dealing with consolidated accounts.

Problems of further expansion of IFRS

IFRS are only required for a small number of German companies, approximately 1,500. Compared to the larger number of roughly 3 million non-listed companies, which prepare separate or consolidated financial statements, German GAAP appears to be the predominant GAAP at present and should continue to be so in future. Because of the number of functions a separate financial statement has to fulfil (profit distribution, serving as a base for tax accounting and information), IFRS are not applicable to these statements for the time being; however, there are discussions about splitting up these contradictory functions by establishing a separate tax accounting law or implementing other means of determining distributable profits (such as the solvency test).

While these discussions are still at a relatively early stage, other measures to update German GAAP are being taken in the meantime. The explicit objective of the legislator is to develop German GAAP into an information-oriented accounting system, harmonizing the requirements in accordance with IFRS.[21]

In addition, most companies do not yet see the benefits of converging to IFRS, which is perceived as a voluminous and complex set of accounting standards. There are major concerns –

---

[21] The legislator plans to publish a draft law, the Accounting Modernization Act, later in 2006.

in particular in small and medium-sized enterprises (SMEs) – as to the applicability of these standards, which are intended to serve the purposes of capital-market investors. The IASB has considered these concerns and responded by setting up a project to develop an IFRS for SMEs.[22] In addition to national developments, this could enhance and accelerate the expansion of IFRS, contributing to the harmonization of accounting regulations in Germany. So far, SMEs are not very supportive of a possible IFRS for SMEs due to the additional benefits that separate financial statements prepared in accordance with national GAAP provide (they are multi-purpose financial statements).

Enforcement of IFRS

Enforcement through audit requirements – application of international standards of auditing (ISAs)

In principle, the requirements of the Commercial Code (presented in sect. II.2 of the present chapter) have to be applied. However, with the adoption of standardized accounting provisions, the need for standardized audit requirements has evolved. In contrast to internationally harmonized accounting standards, standardized auditing requirements were only recently discussed and developed. The international organizations involved in this development are the International Federation of Accountants (IFAC) and its International Auditing and Assurance Standards Board (IAASB), which are developing and issuing international standards of auditing (ISAs). Both the relevant German organizations, the Chamber of Public Accountants and the Institute of Public Accountants in Germany (see sect. II) are members of IFAC.

To date, the Institute of Public Accountants has transformed ISAs into national auditing standards. However, the recent EU directive[23] on statutory audits of annual accounts and consolidated accounts stipulates that member States must require statutory auditors and audit firms to carry out statutory audits in compliance with ISAs. The European Commission – in accordance with the procedure specified by the European Council[24] – will have to adopt these ISAs. It is probable that the German Commercial Code will soon incorporate a reference to ISAs. In compliance with the EU directive, additional national auditing standards will apply if they cover subject matters for which the Commission has not adopted ISAs. [25]

Enforcement through supervisory bodies (Financial Reporting Enforcement Panel and Federal Financial Supervisory Authority)

The legal requirements on securities or stock exchange regulation of the European member States are lacking consistency at the moment. In addition, the corporate governance structures of companies differ significantly throughout Europe. Due to these differences in legal requirements and companies' structures, a pan-EU enforcement institution does not seem feasible at the moment. Nevertheless, it is believed that harmonization of enforcement systems throughout the EU is an effective tool to create an efficient capital market and a level playing-field within the EU. To this end, the IAS Regulation states that "a proper and rigorous enforcement regime is key

---

[22] See www.iasb.org for a full project report.

[23] Directive of the European Parliament and of the Council of 17 May 2006 (2006/43/EC). *OJ L 157*. 9 June 2006: 87; art. 26 No. 1 of the directive.

[24] Known as the Comitology Process. See Council Decision of 28 June 1999 (1999/468/EC). *OJ L 184*. 17 July 1999: 23. The Comitology Process is also applied to adopt IFRS.

[25] For example, guidance on auditing a management report.

to underpinning investors' confidence in financial markets … The Commission intends to liaise with Member States, notably through the Committee of European Securities Regulators to develop a common approach to enforcement."[26]

The principles on the structure of national enforcement institutions as laid out in Committee of European Securities Regulators standard No. 1[27] were implemented in German law in 2004 through the Accounting Enforcement Act.[28] This act's fundamental approach is a two-tier enforcement system.

The first tier is the German Financial Reporting Enforcement Panel, a private institution. In accordance with the article 342b of the Commercial Code, representatives of 15 professional and industry associations,[29] headed by the Federal Ministry of Justice, founded the Financial Reporting Enforcement Panel, which is to serve as the sponsoring organization for an independent body (panel) enforcing financial reporting requirements in listed entities. Next, 12 members of the panel were elected and appointed. The appointed members had to satisfy high job specifications with regard to expertise, experience, independence and integrity. The panel operates under a president and vice-president, both of whom are distinguished accounting experts in Germany. By law, funding provisions must also be made. Since all entities listed[30] on a national stock exchange are subject to examination by the enforcement panel, all of these entities are required to contribute to funding the Financial Reporting Enforcement Panel.[31]

The panel examines both consolidated financial statements and separate financial statements of entities listed in Germany. But the national legislator has recently published a draft law to implement the requirements of the European Transparency Directive. Article 24 (4) (h) of the Transparency Directive requires EU member States to enforce all reporting requirements within the directive. The draft law therefore proposes half-yearly financial statements to be subject to enforcement. This would significantly broaden the range of functions of the Financial Reporting Enforcement Panel.

The enforcement panel shall conduct its examination:
– If there are concrete indications of an infringement of financial reporting requirements, including IFRS; this may also include complaints brought forward by whistle-blowers (motivated audit);
– Upon request by the Federal Financial Supervisory Authority; or
– Without any particular reason (regular sampling audit).

If non-conformity with accounting standards is detected, the panel is asked to seek a solution together with the entity under examination. If, however, intentional infringements or even violations are discovered, the panel is to advise the Federal Financial Supervisory Authority– the second tier of the enforcement structure – of the result of its examination. Under article 342b of the Commercial Code, the panel does not have any authority to impose sanctions; its remit is solely to uncover infringements of financial reporting requirements by listed entities.

---

[26] See recital No. 16 of the IAS Regulation.

[27] So far, the Committee of European Securities Regulators has published two standards, the first of which establishes minimum requirements with regard to the organization, competencies and methods of enforcement by which harmonization on the institutional oversight systems in Europe may be achieved. Standard No. 2 relates to financial information coordination of enforcement activities.

[28] Accounting Enforcement Act.

[29] At present, 17 associations are registered Financial Reporting Enforcement Panel members.

[30] This includes both issuers of equity and issuers of debt.

[31] There is a range for the amount to be contributed by the entities, from a minimum of € 250 to a maximum of € 15 000 per year, depending on the annual turnover of the entity.

The Financial Reporting Enforcement Panel has to report to Federal Financial Supervisory Authority on the overall volume and the results of its examinations. Aside from these general reports, the Federal Financial Supervisory Authority – as the second tier – is only called upon when further action is needed. The Federal Financial Supervisory Authority must take further action if the panel discovers infringements or in case of non-cooperation of the entity (no correction of the erroneous accounting policy) under examination. Being a federal authority, the Federal Financial Supervisory Authority (and the Federal Financial Supervisory Authority alone) is authorized to impose sanctions upon the entities. It is believed that combining private and public elements in a two-tier structure demonstrates that the best expertise can be brought together when dealing with ever more complex issues of financial reporting.

Financial Reporting Enforcement Panel's first report outlines its work in 2005, which began on 1 July 2005. During the second half of 2005, a total of seven motivated audits and 43 regular sampling audits were conducted. All entities examined agreed to cooperate with the enforcement panel. Three of the motivated audits and four of the regular sampling audits were completed in 2005. In two cases, non-compliance with accounting requirements was discovered. One of those entities was instructed by the Federal Financial Supervisory Authority to announce the non-compliance. The other case is still pending, as the relevant institutions are assessing whether the entity can rightly claims a legitimate interest in refraining from the announcement. The Chamber of Public Accountants (see sect. I) was informed that an ineligible auditor may have been elected. The Financial Reporting Enforcement Panel intends to conduct 120 to 160 audits per year.

In general, enforcement aims at ensuring a consistent application of IFRS. Inherent in every accounting system is the problem of possible lack of regulation: since no single set of accounting standards can address every existing or possible accounting issue, standards requiring further interpretation or regulatory gaps related to issues not covered by a specific accounting standard are inevitable. Therefore, enforcement institutions often have to interpret the relevant accounting standards to evaluate whether the standards have been appropriately applied. Consequently, in addition to uncovering infringements and taking appropriate measures, enforcement institutions also interpret existing accounting standards.

However, the Committee of European Securities Regulators advises national enforcement institutions not to publish national interpretations or guidelines, but to forward the issue to the International Financial Reporting Interpretations Committee (IFRIC) or the IASB for clarification, an approach strongly supported by the German enforcement institutions. Accounting issues that arise are to be discussed at the recently established EU round table. The round table is coordinated by the Accounting Regulatory Committee and aims to promote a consistent application of IFRS. If applicable, the accounting issues are referred to IFRIC.

To ensure a uniform application of accounting standards throughout the EU, the Committee of European Securities Regulators introduced a database of enforcement decisions. These former decisions ought to be considered for future cases to allow for consistent enforcement over time.[32]

---

[32] Moreover, it is planned to open up the database to other interested parties such as auditors, auditing companies, preparers or securities regulators outside of Europe.

IV. Issues regarding the transition to international financial reporting standards in Germany

Developments in the transition to IFRS

As mentioned in section II, IAS became relevant when German companies were being listed on the New York Stock Exchange (United States GAAP) and dual consolidated financial statements (Commercial Code/IFRS). In 1997, 20 per cent of the 30 companies listed on the German Primary Index (DAX-30)[33] were already publishing financial statements in accordance with IFRS, while 10 per cent of the companies listed on this index published financial statements in accordance with United States GAAP. The following table gives an overview of how the situation evolved, until the year 2000 when the EU announced its intention to make IFRS mandatory for all listed companies preparing consolidated financial statements. The numbers demonstrate that German companies had favoured IFRS even prior to the EU announcement.

Figure 3. Accounting systems applied by DAX-30 companies until 2000

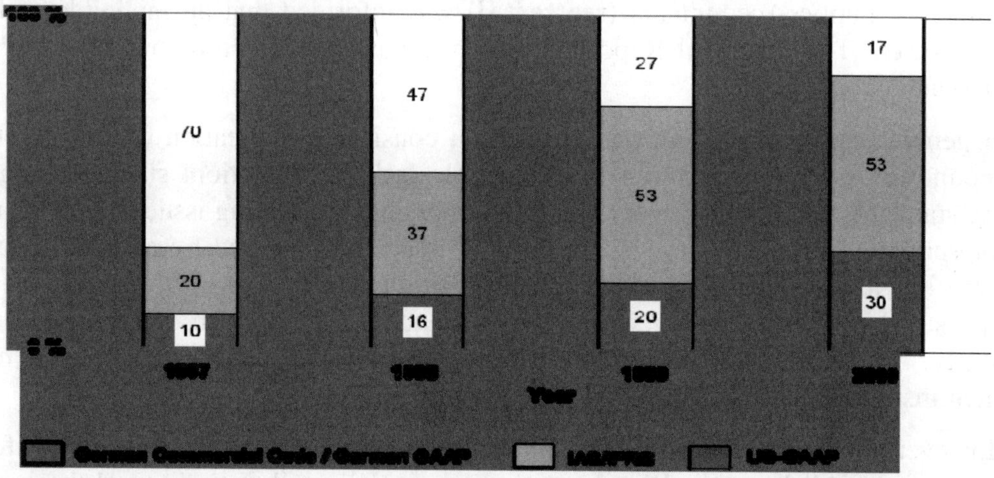

For the decision on the international accounting system companies took the factors, among others, into consideration:

- European and national influence on IFRS standard-setting process (no influence on United States GAAP, which are a form of national GAAP);
- Explicit options under IFRS;
- IFRS closer to German GAAP;
- IFRS more principle-oriented than rule-based United States GAAP; IFRS therefore less detailed.

United States GAAP is mostly appropriate for companies seeking a listing on a United States stock exchange or if their business activities are focused on the United States market. The IAS Regulation states that companies applying United States GAAP would have to perform another transition: from United States GAAP to IFRS (effective for financial years starting 1

---

[33] This index was developed in 1988 and encompasses Germany's 30 largest-volume and most actively traded stocks. The DAX-30 is the leading index of the German stock exchange.

January 2007). Therefore, for those companies listed in the United States, there is potentially a risk of having to prepare multiple financial statements and reconcile from IFRS to United States GAAP, as IFRS are currently not accepted by the Security Exchange Commission. As a result, the convergence programme of both the Financial Accounting Standards Board of the United States and the IASB[34] and the efforts to achieve mutual acceptance are extremely relevant for the German companies.

In 2002, when the IAS Regulation was published, about 36 per cent of all group companies required to prepare IFRS consolidated financial statements by article 4 of that regulation were applying already IFRS.[35] When compared to the total of 5 per cent (350 out of about 7000) of all European companies addressed by article 4 of the IAS Regulation, German companies were evidently ahead of most other European companies.[36] After the adoption of the IAS Regulation the application of accounting systems was spread as illustrated in figure 4:

Figure 4. Accounting systems applied by German subject to article 4 of the IAS Regulation

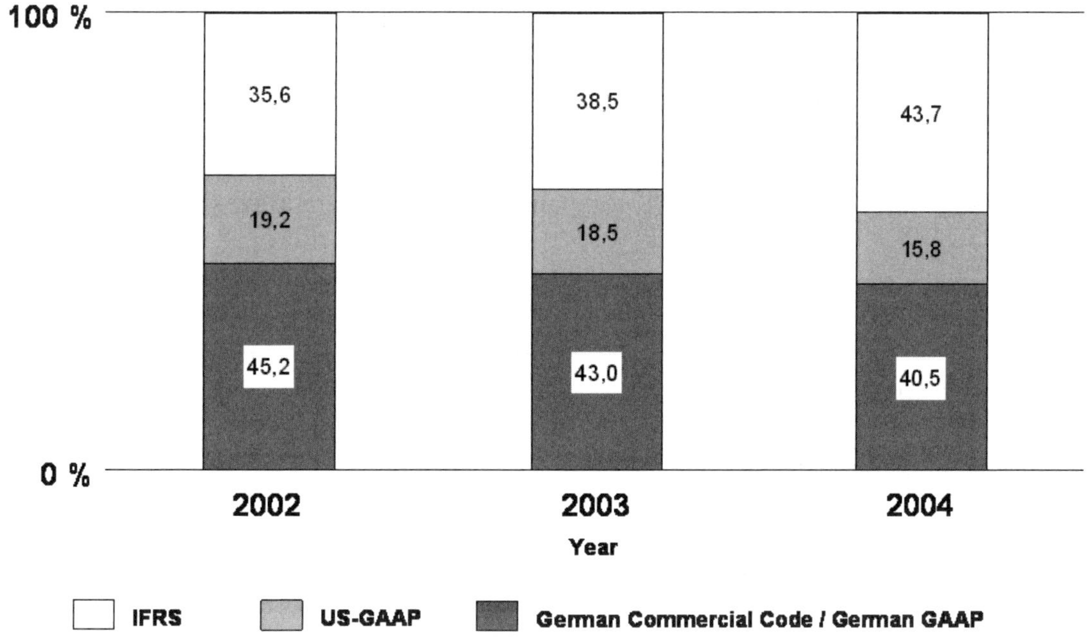

Procedure of transition to IFRS

The transition to IFRS is a complex procedure which does not affect the accounting department of a company alone. It is to be carefully planned and implemented. Figure 5 illustrates a possible breakdown into six phases.

---

[34] The roadmap for developing common accounting standards by 2008 was published on 27 February 2006.
[35] 45 per cent of those companies were still applying German GAAP.
[36] See *IAS/IFRS – Capital market oriented companies in Germany*. 2004: 6–7.

Figure 5. Possible phases of a transition process

Erreur !

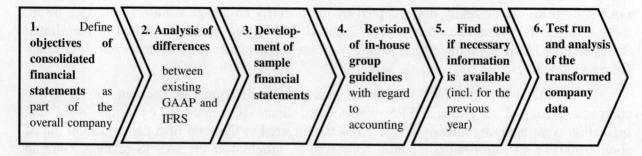

| 1. Define objectives of consolidated financial statements as part of the overall company | 2. Analysis of differences between existing GAAP and IFRS | 3. Development of sample financial statements | 4. Revision of in-house group guidelines with regard to accounting | 5. Find out if necessary information is available (incl. for the previous year) | 6. Test run and analysis of the transformed company data |

In 2004, a survey[37] of 88 companies listed on the Frankfurt Stock Exchange showed that on average companies needed 5.7 months to plan the conversion and 7.7 months to implement the new accounting standards.[38] Overall, a total of 12–18 months should be allowed to complete the transition process. In addition to the one-time costs of the conversion, the recurring costs of applying the new accounting standards must be considered. The following are illustrations of main sectors subject to increased costs occurring during the process of conversion:

– Hiring and training of staff, coordination with external consultants;
– Information-technology reorganization, revision of in-house guidelines and costs of test-run.

The greatest proportion of the conversion costs are expenses for knowledgeable staff and adjustments of accounting-related information technology systems. Table 1 gives an overview of major conversion expenditures incurred in 88 companies of the German prime standard:[39]

Table 1. Major cost components of transformation process

Cost component	Average expenditure (1 000 euro)
In-house staff	255.52
Information technology	247.62
External consultants	154.20
Training	59.47
Total Costs	**716.81**

All companies agreed that it is crucial for a successful implementation project to provide sufficient financial resources and staff during the conversion process.

---

[37] Research conducted by Deloitte. *Turning away from German GAAP – Accounting Transition Experiences, from German GAAP to IFRS or US-GAAP.* 2004: 9.

[38] These data show a high statistical spread; therefore, average numbers are only approximate.

[39] See Deloitte, *op. cit.*, 2004: 12.

Implication of the transition for financial reporting statements

A general statement about the effect of the conversion of the accounting system to IFRS cannot be given, because of the opposing effects on separate positions. Nevertheless, any impact on the presented company profit represents a one-time-only effect. The value of net assets or the financial position of a company will not constantly be higher or lower compared to national GAAP. Any impact of the accounting transition signifies only temporary changes. Substantial differences between German GAAP and IFRS consist, for example, in the following cases:

Table 2. Impact of IFRS on the presentation of profit and loss and equity

	P & L	Equity
Capitalisation of Development Cost	⬆	⬆
Non-Amortisation of Goodwill	⬆	⬆
Change of Depreciation Methods	⬆	⬆
Reclassification of Leases	—	—
Fair Value Measurement of Securities and Derivatives	⬆⬇	⬆⬇
Changes in Measuring Inventory	⬆	⬆
Change in Recognition of Provisions	⬆	⬆
Increase in Pension Liabilities	⬇	⬇
Comprehensive Recognition of Deferred Taxes	⬆⬇	⬆⬇
Consolidation of SPEs	⬆⬇	—

In table 2, the arrows and the horizontal line are used to indicate decrease, increase and no change in the profit and loss and equity of an entity caused by the transition to IFRS. Where two directions are indicated, an increase or a decrease on profit and loss or equity could result, depending on the specific circumstances of the entity transitioning to IFRS.

Major technical issue: Classification of equity and debt

The major issue concerning the application of IFRS by German companies is the differing classification of equity and liabilities. This has an extremely problematic impact on the balance sheet, namely significant reduction of equity. As a result, it appears to be the main obstacle to overall acceptance of IFRS in Germany. The distinction between equity and liabilities according to IAS 32 follows an approach based on the existence of an obligation of the entity. Therefore, any instruments that are repayable within the lifetime of the entity are classified as liabilities. But the term "obligation" encompasses both present and contingent obligations. Therefore, if an instrument is repayable at the option of the holder (the holder has a right to put the instrument back to the entity), this instrument will also be classified as a liability. Even if the put option is exercisable in a number of years or if the put option has a remote probability of being exercised, this would not change the liability classification.

Under German GAAP, however, other criteria are important for the classification. As German accounting aims at capital maintenance, risk capital remaining with the entity even for a short period of time will be classified as equity. To be classified as equity, the capital must be

41

loss-absorbing, and it must be subordinated to straight debt on liquidation. In contrast to IAS 32, the capital may be repayable or the instrument may be puttable by the holder. For example, every member in a private partnership has a legal right to quit the partnership and the law grants the member the right to put back his or her share. As a consequence of this legal right German private partnerships may not present equity in their financial statements if prepared under IFRS. As the legal form of the partnership is quite common in Germany for all types of businesses, including for subsidiaries of listed companies, this IFRS implementation issue is of great importance. In addition, cooperative societies are affected, as their members also have the legal right to put back their shares.

Some hybrid instruments which may be classified as equity under German GAAP would be classified as debt under IAS 32. At present, the IASB is discussing possibilities for granting exemptions for certain kinds of capital instruments which would undoubtedly be classified as debt under current the principle of IAS 32. The exposure draft deals with instruments puttable at fair value. Since they are puttable, there is a contingent obligation for the entity to repay the instrument. Nevertheless, there are additional criteria which cannot be fulfilled due to legal peculiarities of some partnerships, for example, such as those in Germany. Therefore, this exposure draft will arguably not solve German companies' equity problem. This exposure draft is regarded as a short-term solution by the IASB. In addition, the IASB and the FASB are currently working on a joint project dealing with a completely new distinction between equity and debt. Preliminary views are not expected before 2007.

The ASCG is also working on the issue and trying to develop an alternative approach to IAS 32. The GASB has also set up a working group comprising of academics, practitioners and auditors. Furthermore, the ASCG is the project leader of the working group of the European Financial Reporting Advisory Group on the same issue, under the Proactive Accounting in Europe initiative.

V. Conclusion and outlook

When looking back on the developments of the past two decades, a tremendous change to the German accounting environment is evident. As a result of globalization and internationalization of the business environment and increasing demand to access capital markets outside of Germany, alternatives to traditional German GAAP had become necessary. The initial European strategy for harmonized accounting regulations through convergence of national requirements did not succeed fully in meeting the needs of companies that wished to raise capital on pan-European or international securities markets. Regardless of a lack of legal requirements to do so, many capital market-oriented companies turned towards internationally accepted accounting standards, driven by general economic conditions.

Significant differences between financial statements prepared under IAS and financial statements prepared in accordance with German GAAP were revealed. As German GAAP was designed and perceived to be creditor-oriented and therefore ruled by the prudence principle, DaimlerChrysler's profit had decreased under United States GAAP by € 1.3 billion. A negative impact on the profit was obviously contrary to the strong emphasis on prudence, which suggested hidden reserves. This particular effect resulted from a lack of recognition and lower measurement of pension-benefit plans.

Nevertheless, it was difficult to communicate the causes of such differences in the annual accounts. From an international investor's perspective, German GAAP with its strong emphasis on a prudence principle was looked upon as incompatible with value-oriented financial reporting.[40] German GAAP did not attempt to compete with other accounting systems for international acceptance. In the light of obvious shortcomings, the many merits of the systems remained unnoticed.

German capital-market-oriented companies were exposed to burdensome, cost-intensive dual accounting, until the German legislator allowed consolidated financial statements to be prepared following internationally accepted accounting standards. This decision was confirmed by the European legislator in the IAS Regulation of 2002.

At present, multiple accounting systems coexist, the inefficiency of which is obvious from an economical point of view. Therefore the challenge lies in:

- – Enhancing acceptance of IFRS;
- – Exploring further possibilities to open up separate financial statements to IFRS.

When converting to IFRS, companies have to: (1) gain knowledge of a fundamentally different accounting system; (2) apply more complex accounting standards with an increasing tendency to market valuation; and (3) cope with constant changes of the accounting regulation. In 1998, German legislators decided to allow listed companies to prepare consolidated financial statements in accordance with internationally accepted standards (IFRS or United States GAAP). Thus, listed companies in Germany embarked on the implementation of IFRS many years ahead of other entities outside Germany. For example, most listed entities in the European Union began the process in response to the IAS Regulation that became effective in 2005. As a result, German listed companies had relatively more time to adopt IFRS and to build up the necessary resources. The capacity-building process in the form of establishing public and private accounting and enforcement institutions has helped to set the frame for German GAAP that is increasingly becoming internationalized.

---

[40] The provisions with regard to pension-benefit plans, which admitted that all liabilities need not be recognized and measured at lower than market value, were seen by international investors as a crucial shortcoming of German GAAP.

Chapter IV

Case study of India

I. Introduction[41]

In recent years, India has experienced strong economic growth, rising foreign exchange reserves, falling inflation, global recognition of its technological competence and interest shown by many developed countries to invest in the engineers and scientists produced in the country, including by setting up of new research and development centres. Above all, as the largest democracy in the world, India has a reputation for providing leadership for one billion people in a country with different cultures, languages and religions. The technological competence and value systems of India are highly respected. Foreign institutional investors find investing in India attractive. Indians are also investing in companies abroad and are opening new business ventures. The Government of India is also committed to economic development, ensuring a growth rate of 7–8 per cent annually, enhancing the welfare of farmers and workers and unlocking the creativity of the entrepreneurs, business persons, scientists, engineers and other productive forces of the society. Today, India is one of the fastest growing economies in the world, with a compounded average growth rate of 5.7 per cent over the past two decades. The Government of India has plans to transform India into a developed nation by 2020.

In India, accounting standards are issued by the Institute of Chartered Accountants of India based on international financial reporting standards (IFRS). Departures from IFRS are made with a view to the prevailing legal position and customs and usages in the country. Accordingly, this case study of India is prepared to highlight the practical challenges involved in adapting IFRS in India. This case study also throws light on the existing regulatory framework in the country and the enforcement of the standards in the country.

Accounting standards-setting in India: A historical perspective

The accounting profession in India was among the earliest to develop, as the Indian Companies Act was introduced in the mid-1800s, giving the accounting profession its start. Since then, considerable efforts have been made to align Indian accounting and auditing standards and practices with internationally accepted standards. Indian accounting and auditing standards are developed on the basis of international standards and the country has many accountants and auditors who are highly skilled and capable of providing international-standard services.

The Institute of Chartered Accountants of India (ICAI) set up the Accounting Standards Board in 1977 to prepare accounting standards. In 1982, ICAI set up the Auditing and Assurance Standards Board (initially known as the Auditing Practice Committee) to prepare auditing standards. ICAI became one of the associate members of the International Accounting Standards

---

[41] This chapter was prepared and edited by the UNCTAD secretariat with substantive inputs from Avinash Chander, Institute of Chartered Accountants of India.

Committee (IASC) in June 1973. ICAI also became a member of the International Federation of Accountants (IFAC) at its inception in October 1977. While formulating accounting standards in India, the ASB considers IFRS and tries to integrate them, to the extent possible, in the light of the prevailing laws, customs, practices and business environment in India.

The Accounting Standards Board has worked hard to introduce an overall qualitative improvement in the financial reporting in the country by formulating accounting standards to be followed in the preparation and presentation of financial statements. So far, the board has issued 29 accounting standards. In addition, it has also issued various accounting standards interpretations and announcements, so as to ensure uniform application of accounting standards and to provide guidance on the issues concerning the implementation of accounting standards which may be of general relevance. Appendix A contains a comparative statement of international accounting standards/international financial reporting standards and Indian accounting standards.

As accounting standards in India are formulated on the basis of IFRS issued by the IASB, ICAI interacts with the IASB at various levels, namely:

- Sending comments on the various draft IFRS issued by the IASB;
- Active participation in the meetings of the global standard-setters with the IASB;
- Active participation in the meetings of the regional standard-setters with the IASB;
- Contribution in the discussions on various ongoing projects of the IASB, e.g. on the IASB management commentary project;
- ICAI is approaching the IASB to take up projects to be carried on by India, e.g. IFRS for regulated enterprises.

II. Regulatory framework and enforcement of accounting standards

In the following paragraphs, the regulatory framework of financial reporting and enforcement of accounting standards will be discussed.

(A) Legal Recognition of accounting standards issued by ICAI under the Companies Act (1956)

The Companies Act (1956) provides the basic requirements for financial reporting of all companies in India. The Act requires the preparation, presentation, publication, and disclosure of financial statements, as well as an audit of all companies by a member-in-practice certified by the Institute of Chartered Accountants of India (ICAI). Under the Act, the Central Government has the power, by notification in the *Official Gazette*, to constitute the National Advisory Committee on Accounting Standards to advise the Central Government on the formulation and laying down of accounting standards for adoption by companies or class of companies. For this purpose, the Act requires the committee to consider accounting standards issued by ICAI when recommending accounting standards to the Government. While, as stated earlier, ICAI bases its accounting standards on the corresponding IAS/IFRS, the committee also specifically considers any deviations from– and reasons, if any, for them – the corresponding IAS/IFRS when reviewing ICAI accounting standards. Where the committee is not satisfied by any deviation, it requests ICAI to amend the standard to comply with IFRS. ICAI generally deviates from the corresponding IAS/IFRS because of the following factors:

- Legal and regulatory environment prevailing in the country;
- Alternatives permitted in IFRS would lead to incomparable financial information;
- Economic environment within the country;
- Level of preparedness of industry.

The committee has recommended to the Government all 29 accounting standards issued by ICAI, with the exception of accounting standard No. 8 on accounting for research and development (which has already been withdrawn pursuant to accounting standard No. 26 on intangible assets), which will become mandatory for notification under the Companies Act (1956). These include the revised accounting standard No. 15on employee benefits, recently issued by ICAI in line with IAS 19 on employee benefits. Notification by the Government of these standards is expected shortly. Until then, the Companies Act (1956) specifically provides that companies must adhere to ICAI accounting standards.

(B)   Legal recognition of accounting standards by other regulators

Reserve Bank of India

The Reserve Bank of India was established to regulate the issue of banknotes and the keeping of reserves to secure monetary stability in India, as well as to generally operate the currency and credit system of the country to advantage. The Banking Regulation Act (1949) empowers the bank to regulate financial reporting of the financial sector, including banks and financial institutions. One of the schedules to the Banking Regulation Act prescribes formats for general-purpose financial statements (e.g. balance sheet, and profit and loss accounts) and other disclosure requirements. Banks are also required to comply with the requirements of the Companies Act (1956), provided that they are consistent with the Banking Regulation Act. The Reserve Bank has issued circulars requiring banks to comply with the accounting standards issued by ICAI.

Securities and Exchange Board of India

The Securities and Exchange Board of India Act protects investors and regulates the securities market. Listed companies in India are required to comply with the requirements prescribed by the board in its 1992 Act and the Securities Contracts (Regulation) Act of 1956, which provides for the regulation of securities transactions. To protect investor interests, the board has issued a listing agreement which specifies disclosures applicable to listed companies, in addition to other applicable auditing and accounting requirements. In particular, it requires compliance with the accounting standards issued by ICAI.

The Insurance Regulatory and Development Authority

The Insurance Regulatory and Development Authority regulates the financial reporting practices of insurance companies under the Insurance Regulatory and Development Authority Act (1999). This authority has been constituted to regulate, promote and ensure orderly growth of the insurance business and reinsurance business. Insurance companies and their auditors are required to comply with the requirements of the authority's 2002 regulations, entitled "Preparation of Financial Statements and Auditor's Report of the Insurance Companies", when preparing and presenting their financial statements and the format and content of the audit report. The authority's regulations require compliance with the accounting standards issued by ICAI.

The Institute of Chartered Accountants of India as a regulator

ICAI requires its members to ensure compliance with all the accounting standards that it issues while discharging their attesting function. Further, ICAI members are required to follow a detailed code of ethics, as prescribed under the Chartered Accountants Act (1949). The ICAI council is also entrusted with the disciplinary powers that are exercised through its disciplinary committee. Recently, extensive changes have been introduced into the Act through the Chartered Accountants (Amendment) Act (2006), which has made the ICAI disciplinary mechanism more stringent.

ICAI, with a view to further improving and strengthening financial reporting practices in India, has also constituted the Financial Reporting Review Board. The board reviews general-purpose financial statements of certain selected enterprises with a view to ensuring compliance with, inter alia, the accounting standards. In cases, where non-compliance is observed, appropriate action is taken by ICAI and/or the case is referred to an appropriate authority for the action. This step definitely helps improve the quality of financial reporting in the country.

ICAI introduced a peer review of audit firms by establishing an 11-member peer review board in March 2002. The peer review board provides guidance on enhancing the quality of services provided by ICAI members. In the first phase, peer review focuses on the review of firms that audit major enterprises at least once in a three-year period. The peer review does not lead to any disciplinary or regulatory mechanism. Peer review certification is either given or not given according to the findings of the review. Peer reviewers are practitioners with at least 15 years' audit experience.

The Chartered Accountants (Amendment) Act (2006) created a quality review board to replace of the peer review board; the new board will be make recommendations to the ICAI council on the formulation of standards regarding the quality of services provided by the members. Further, the proposed quality review board would also review the quality of services provided by ICAI members, including audit services, and guide ICAI members in improving the quality of services and compliance with the various statutory and other regulatory requirements.

Challenges involved in adoption of IFRS and implementation issues

(A)   Convergence with IFRS in India

A financial reporting system supported by strong governance, high-quality standards and a sound regulatory framework is key to economic development. Indeed, high-quality standards of financial reporting, auditing and ethics form the foundations of the trust that investors place in financial information and therefore play an integral role in contributing to a country's economic growth and financial stability. As the forces of globalization prompt more and more countries to open their doors to foreign investment and as businesses expand across borders, both the public and private sectors are increasingly recognizing the benefits of having a commonly understood financial reporting framework, supported by strong globally accepted standards. The benefits of a global financial reporting framework are numerous and include:

- Greater comparability of financial information for investors;

- Greater willingness on the part of investors to invest across borders;
- Lower cost of capital;
- More efficient allocation of resources; and
- Greater economic growth.

However, before these benefits can be fully realized, there must be greater convergence with a single set of globally accepted high-quality standards. International convergence is a goal that is embraced in the mission of the International Federation of Accountants (IFAC) and shared by IFAC members, international standard-setters and many national standard-setters.

As a member body of IFAC, India has recognized in its preface to the statements of accounting standards that "ICAI, being a full-fledged member of the International Federation of Accountants (IFAC), is expected, inter alia, to actively promote the International Accounting Standards Board's (IASB) pronouncements in the country with a view to facilitating global harmonization of accounting standards. Accordingly, while formulating the accounting standards, the Accounting Standards Board will give due consideration to International Accounting Standards (IAS) issued by the International Accounting Standards Committee (predecessor body to the IASB) or international financial reporting standards (IFRS) issued by the IASB, as the case may be, and try to integrate them, to the extent possible, in the light of the conditions and practices prevailing in India".

Accordingly, the accounting standards issued by ICAI are generally in conformity with IFRS. Indeed, with respect to certain recently issued/revised Indian accounting standards, there are no differences between the Indian accounting standards and IFRS. For example, accounting standard No. 7 on construction contracts and accounting standard 28 on impairment of assets are identical to the corresponding IFRS. However, in exceptional cases, when a departure from IFRS is warranted by conditions in India, the major areas of difference between the two are pointed out in the appendix to the accounting standard.

ICAI endeavours to bridge the gap between Indian accounting standards and IFRS by issuing new accounting standards and ensuring that existing Indian accounting standards reflect any changes in international thinking on various accounting issues. In this regard, it should be noted that ICAI is making a conscious effort to bring the Indian accounting standards into line with IFRS by revising existing accounting standards. ICAI has so far issued 29 Indian accounting standards corresponding to IFRS.

In view of the above, Indian accounting standards are largely in step with IFRS. This is also recognized in the following extracts of article from an Indian financial daily, *Hindu Business Line*, on 5 November 2005:

"Indian Companies can now get listed on the London Stock Exchange (LSE) by reporting their financial results based on Indian accounting standards. Until now, these companies had to report their financial data in accordance with the international financial reporting standards (IFRS)."

This is an indication of the growing convergence of Indian accounting standards with IFRS.

(B) Challenges and issues involved in convergence with IFRS in India

Legal and regulatory considerations

In some cases, the legal and regulatory accounting requirements in India differ from the IFRS; in such cases, strict adherence to IFRS in India would result in various legal problems. The examples below illustrate this point.

IAS 1 – Presentation of Financial Statements

In India, laws governing companies (e.g. the Companies Act of 1956), banking enterprises (e.g. the Banking Regulation Act of 1949) and insurance enterprises (formats of financial statements for insurance companies as prescribed by the Insurance Regulatory and Development Authority regulations in the document "Preparation of Financial Statements and Auditor's Report of the Insurance Companies" (2002), prescribes detailed formats for financial statements to be followed by respective enterprises. At this stage lawmakers/regulators may not be willing to accept IAS 1 in its present form and change the existing law. Therefore, full adoption of IAS 1 may not be possible at this stage. However, it is proposed that the corresponding accounting standard being developed by ICAI, would have an appendix containing suggested detailed formats of financial statements which, while complying with IAS 1, would also contain other disclosures prescribed in the formats laid down by various legislations to address the concerns of the legislature.

IAS 21 – The Effects of Changes in Foreign Exchange Rates

If IAS 21 is adopted in India it would result in violation of schedule VI to the Companies Act of 1956. Schedule VI requires foreign currency fluctuations in respect of foreign currency loans raised to acquiring foreign assets to be reflected in the cost of the fixed assets, whereas IAS 21 requires the same to be charged to the profit and loss account. The corresponding Indian accounting standard prescribes the accounting treatment contained in IAS 21; however, through a separate announcement issued by ICAI, it is recognized that law will prevail.

IAS 34 – Interim Financial Reporting

The disclosures requirements of IAS 34 are not in accordance with the formats of unaudited quarterly/half-yearly results prescribed in the listing agreement issued by the Securities and Exchange Board of India. The corresponding Indian standard prescribes disclosure as per IAS 34, but also recognizes that the law will prevail insofar as presentation and disclosure requirements are concerned.

Alternative treatment

IFRS allow alternative treatments a number of cases. The implications of adopting IFRS as they are would be that it would lead to presentation of incomparable financial information by various enterprises. The following examples illustrate this aspect:

IAS 23 – Borrowing Costs

IAS 23 on borrowing costs prescribes expensing of borrowing costs as the benchmark treatment; however, it also allows capitalization of borrowing costs as an allowed alternative. If this standard is followed (and it is), some enterprises then charge borrowing costs to the profit and loss account, while others capitalize these costs as part of the cost of the assets acquired/constructed using the borrowings. In India, however, the corresponding accounting standard No. 16 does not allow any alternative and borrowing costs directly attributable to the acquisition, construction or production of a qualifying asset to be capitalized. However, the IASB has issued an exposure draft of proposed amendments to IAS 23 in May 2006, in which it has decided to eliminate the option of immediate recognition of the borrowings costs as an expense and allow only capitalization of borrowing costs that are directly attributable to the acquisition, construction or production of a qualifying asset as part of the cost of the assets. Thus, once this exposure draft is finalized, no difference would remain between accounting standard No. 16 and IAS 23.

IAS 19 – Employee Benefits

IAS 19 allows the following options with regard to the treatment of actuarial gains and losses:

- Immediate recognition in the profit and loss account in the year in which such gains and losses occur;
- Adjustment against the retained earnings, whereby the current year's profit and loss account is not affected at all; or
- Recognition of a part of the actuarial gains and losses in the profit and loss account which exceeds the specified percentage (known as the "corridor approach").

The corresponding Indian accounting standard No. 15 on employee benefits requires only the first alternative, however: i.e. immediate recognition in the profit and loss account.

The above are only some of the examples that could be presented. To facilitate comparability, it is imperative that there should be no options in the accounting standards, otherwise the investors and other users of financial statements cannot take decisions based on comparable information. Indian accounting standards do not ordinarily permit any option, but prescribe one of the most appropriate options permitted by the corresponding IAS/IFRS.

The IASB recently issued the "Statement of Best Practice: Working Relationships between the IASB and other Accounting Standard-Setters", which states that removing optional treatments does not mean any non-compliance with IFRS.

Economic environment

The economic environment and trade customs and practices prevailing in India may not, in a few cases, be conducive for adoption of an approach prescribed in an IFRS. For example, in a country whose markets do not have adequate depth and breadth for reliable determination of fair values, it may not be advisable to follow a fair value-based approach prescribed in certain IFRS. Certain IAS/IFRS assume an economic environment with mature markets. For example, IAS 41 on agriculture is based on the fair value approach presuming that fair values are available for various biological assets such as plants, crops and living animals. The standard is relevant only if the fair values are reliable; this may not be true in India as, in some instances, market data may not be reliable in view of markets not being mature enough.

Conceptually, ICAI is in agreement with the fair value approach followed in various IFRS. However, there is always the risk of misuse of this approach as was reportedly the case in Enron. ICAI has so far been cautious in adopting the fair value approach in its accounting standards, although certain accounting standards recognize this approach, (for example, accounting standard No. 28 on impairment of assets), and ICAI has decided to follow this approach in its proposed accounting standard on financial instruments (recognition and measurement) corresponding to IAS 39.

Level of preparedness

In a few cases, the adoption of IFRS may cause hardship to the industry. To avoid the hardship, some companies have gone to the court to challenge the standard, for example:

- When ICAI issued accounting standard No. 19 on leases, which is based on the corresponding IAS, leasing companies are of the view that it may cause hardship to them. To avoid this, the Association of Leasing Companies approached the courts to receive context to the standard.
- When ICAI issued accounting standard No. 22 on accounting for taxes on income to introduce the international concept of deferred taxes in India for the first time, a number of companies challenged the standard in court, as they were concerned about the effect it may have on their bottom lines.

In view of the above, to avoid hardship in some genuine cases, ICAI has deviated from corresponding IFRS for a limited period until such time as preparedness is achieved.

In addition to the above-mentioned technical differences, there are a few conceptual differences between Indian accounting standards and IFRS. For example, IAS 37 deals with constructive obligation in the context of creation of a provision. The effect of recognizing provision on the basis of constructive obligation is that, in some cases, provision will need to be recognized at an early stage. For instance, in case of a restructuring, a constructive obligation arises when an enterprise has a detailed formal plan for the restructuring and the enterprise has raised a valid expectation in those affected that it will carry out the restructuring by starting to implement that plan or announcing its main features to those affected by it. It is felt that merely on the basis of a detailed formal plan and announcement thereof, it would not be appropriate to recognize a provision, since a liability cannot be considered to be crystallized at this stage. Furthermore, the judgment whether the management has raised valid expectations in those affected may be a matter for considerable argument. Accordingly, the corresponding Indian accounting standard, accounting standard No. 29, does not specifically deal with constructive obligation. Accounting standard No. 29 does, however, require a provision to be created in respect of obligations arising from normal business practice, custom and a desire to maintain good business relations or act in an equitable manner. In such cases, general criteria for recognition of provision must be applied. The treatment prescribed in accounting standard No. 29 is also in consonance with the legal requirements in India.

Frequency, volume and complexity of changes to the international financial reporting standards

It has clearly been a very challenging time for preparers, auditors and users of financial statements, following the publication of new and revised IFRS. The following changes evidence the frequency, volume and complexity of the changes to the international standards:

- The IASB Improvements Project resulted in 13 standards being amended, as well as consequential amendments to many others. In India, a project to examine of IAS revisions, pursuant to the IASB improvement project, has been launched to determine whether corresponding Indian accounting standards need revision.
- Repeated changes of the same standards, including changes reversing the previous stances of the IASB, and changes for the purpose of international convergence.
- Complex changes on accounting standards, such as those on financial instruments, impairment of assets and employee benefits, require upgrading of skills of those professionals who implement them, in order to keep up with the changes.

Challenges for small and medium-sized enterprises and accounting firms

In emerging economies like India, a significant part of the economic activities is carried on by small- and medium-sized enterprises (SMEs). SMEs face problems in implementing the accounting standards because:

- Resources and expertise within the SMEs are scarce; and
- Cost of compliance is not commensurate with the expected benefits.

To address the issue of applicability of accounting standards to SMEs, ICAI has provided certain exemptions/relaxations for such companies. For the purpose of applicability of accounting standards, enterprises are classified into three categories: level I, level II and level III. Level I enterprises are large and publicly accountable entities. Level II enterprises are medium-sized enterprises and level III are small enterprises. Level II and level III enterprises are considered as SMEs. Level I enterprises are required to comply fully with all the accounting standards issued by ICAI. The relaxations/exemptions are provided for level II and level III enterprises from accounting standards. Level II and level III enterprises are fully exempted from certain accounting standards which primarily lay down disclosure requirements, such as accounting standard No. 3 on cash flow statements, accounting standard No. 17 on segment reporting, accounting standard No. 18 on related party disclosures and accounting standard No. 24 on discontinuing operations. In respect of certain other accounting standards, which also lay down disclosure requirements, level II and level III enterprises are exempted from some of its disclosure requirements, such as accounting standard No. 19 on leases, accounting standard No. 20 on earnings per share and accounting standard No. 29 on provisions, contingent liabilities and contingent assets. Generally, ICAI does not favour exemptions to be given in respect of recognition and measurement requirements. However, considering rigorous measurement requirements in accounting standard No. 15 (revised 2005) on employee benefits and accounting standard No. 28 on impairment of assets, simplified measurement approaches have been allowed to the SMEs.

III. Capacity-building

The pace at which accounting standards have recently been issued and mandated in India is posing various accounting problems and has serious business consequences. Building the capacity of the preparers and the auditors is therefore a stiff challenge to the accounting profession. To enhance capacity-building and to ensure effective implementation of accounting standards, the Institute of Chartered Accountants has acted proactively by taking the following steps:

(a) *Issuing accounting standards interpretations on matters related to accounting standards*: With a view to resolving various intricate interpretational issues arising in the implementation of new accounting standards that have already been issued, ICAI has issued 30 interpretations of accounting standards.

(b) *Issuance of background materials on accounting standards*: To facilitate discussion at seminars, workshops, etc., ICAI has issued background material on newly issued accounting standards. The background material deals, inter alia, with the key requirements of the accounting standards with examples and frequently asked questions that accountants and auditors may encounter in the application of accounting standards.

(c) *Issuance of guidance notes on accounting matters*: ICAI has issued various guidance notes in order to provide immediate guidance on accounting issues arising as a result of the issuance of new accounting standards, and to provide immediate guidance on new accounting issues arising because of changes in legal or economic environment and/or other developments. These guidance notes form an important part of the generally accepted accounting principles in India and need to be referred to on a regular basis by people involved in the preparation and presentation of financial statements, as well as by people involved in auditing these statements.

(d) *Organizing seminars and workshops*: ICAI has always been striving for excellence in terms of standards of professional services rendered by its members. To enable members to maintain high standards of professional services, ICAI is providing inputs to members by way of seminars, workshops and lectures.

(e) *Responding to various queries raised by members*: While performing their attesting function members of the ICAI are often presented with certain delicate situations, particularly as they apply accounting standards to the specific situations of an enterprise, where an authentic view is required. For the purpose of assisting its members, the ICAI council formed an expert advisory committee to answer queries from its members. The committee deals with queries on accounting and/or auditing principles and related matters.

Auditing issues involved in implementation of accounting standards

Independent auditors play a vital role in enhancing the reliability of financial information produced by companies, not-for-profit organizations, government agencies and other entities by providing assurance on the reliability of the financial statements. As mentioned above, ICAI members are required to ensure compliance with ICAI accounting standards when performing their attesting function under certain legislation (such as the Companies Act (1956)), as well as by ICAI itself.

ICAI has established an auditing and assurance standards board that formulates standards that are broadly in line with ISAs issued by the IAASB. In general, the text of the national board is based on the text of the equivalent ISA, although certain modifications are introduced into the accounting and assurance standards in order to adapt them to local circumstances when considered necessary.

Examples of audit issues arising as a consequence of adaptation of IAS/IFRS

Some of the major issues that may have an impact on the work of auditors in India in implementation of Indian accounting standards that have been formulated on the basis of the corresponding IAS/IFRS are given below.

IAS 8 – Accounting Policies, Changes in Accounting Estimates and Errors

IAS 8 provides that financial statements do not comply with IFRS if they contain immaterial errors that were deliberately included to achieve a particular presentation of an entity's financial position, financial performance or cash flows. The Accounting Standards Board of ICAI has also prepared the preliminary draft of the revised accounting standard No. 5, corresponding to IAS 8. In the draft, the board has decided that since the above accounting treatment is conceptually correct, it should be adopted in accounting standard No. 5 too. However, the board also feels that this requirement would be too onerous on the auditors, since it would be difficult for the auditor to determine whether the errors had been intentionally made or not and he or she may ignore such errors on the grounds of materiality. The board has, therefore, decided that once the standard is finalized, it may ask the Accounting and Assurance Standards Board of ICAI to look into the matter and provide necessary guidance.

IAS 19 - Employee Benefits

IAS 19 also deals with measurement of defined benefit plans, which is complex when compared to measurement of defined contribution plans, since actuarial assumptions are required to measure the obligation and the expense, and there is a possibility of actuarial gains and losses. ICAI has recently issued the revised accounting standard No. 15 on employee benefits based on IAS 19, which recognizes the role of a professional actuary. An auditing issue may arise about the extent of reliance that an auditor may place on the actuary's report, particularly in view of extensive disclosure requirements prescribed in the standard.

To effectively address the problem, ICAI has asked the Actuarial Society of India to revise its guidance note on the subject, so that the actuary's report contains the relevant information as envisaged in the accounting standard, in order to guide actuaries (as has been done in certain other countries, including the United Kingdom). In any case, the responsibility of the auditor will continue to be determined under Auditing and Assurance Standard 9 on using the work of an expert, which provides guidance on auditor's responsibility in relation to and the procedures the auditor should consider in using the work of an expert, such as an actuary, as audit evidence.

IAS 27 – Consolidated and Separate Financial Statements

In accordance with IAS 27, a parent enterprise shall present financial statements in which it consolidates its investments in subsidiaries. Along the lines of IAS 27, IAS 21 on consolidated financial statements provides that a parent which presents consolidated financial statements should consolidate all domestic and foreign subsidiaries.

It is possible that the auditor of the parent enterprise is not the auditor of its subsidiary enterprises. Furthermore, the auditor of the consolidated financial statements may not necessarily be the auditor of the separate financial statements of the parent company, or one or more of the components included in the consolidated financial statements. However, a law or regulation governing the enterprise may require the consolidated financial statements to be audited by the statutory auditor of the enterprise. In such cases, the auditor will face issues of reliability of the work performed by the other auditors. In India, the listing agreement requires financial statements to be audited apart from the audit of separate financial statements under the Companies Act (1956). ICAI recently issued a guidance note on audit of consolidated financial statements, which provides detailed guidance on the specific issues and audit procedures to be applied in an audit of consolidated financial statements.

Fair value issues

Fair value is the amount for which an asset could be exchanged, or a liability settled, between knowledgeable, willing parties in an arm's length transaction. As mentioned in the above section entitled "Challenges involved in adoption of IFRS and implementation issues", the economic environment in India may not be conducive for adoption of the fair value approach prescribed in various IFRS. ICAI agrees on a conceptual level with this approach – it has used it in accounting standard No. 28 on impairment of assets, and has also decided to follow it in its proposed accounting standard No. on financial instruments (recognition and measurement), which corresponds to IAS 39 – but an auditor might face difficulties in satisfying him or herself that the fair values computed are reliable.

Although the IFAC)has recently issued a ISA) on auditing fair value measurements and disclosures to address the increasing number of complex accounting pronouncements containing measurement and disclosure provisions based on fair value, it still remains to be seen whether this ISA, in the Indian context, will adequately address the auditing issues that need to be examined.

IV. Lessons learned

Convergence of accounting standards in all countries, including India, is duly recognized as the future of global accounting standards. In the past, different views of the role of financial reporting made it difficult to encourage convergence of accounting standards, but there now appears to be a growing international consensus that financial reporting should provide high-quality financial information that is comparable, consistent and transparent, in order to serve the needs of investors. Convergence is possible in two ways, either by adopting or adapting a standard. As discussed in earlier sections, IAS and IFRS in India are being adapted while the legal and other conditions prevailing in India are borne in mind. The major lessons learned during such adaptation are:

(1)   Implementation of certain requirements of IFRS should be a gradual process:
India has learned that adapting IFRS is not just an accounting exercise. It is a transition that requires everyone concerned to learn a new language and new way of working. While formulating accounting standards on the basis of IFRS, one should consider that, in certain cases, it may cause undue hardship to the industry, at least at the beginning. In other words, Indian industry may not be prepared to apply the provisions of the standards immediately and some transitional measures are needed to be introduced for them. For example, in the following cases, India has decided to implement accounting standards prepared on the basis of IFRS gradually:

(i) Accounting standard No. 10 (revised) – Tangible Fixed Assets: This standard is being revised on the basis of IAS 16. IAS 16 follows the components approach in accounting for property, plant and equipment. Under this approach, each part of a tangible fixed asset with a cost that is significant in relation to its total cost is depreciated separately. Accounting standard No. 10 (revised) also recognizes the components approach, yet does not at present require full adoption of the said approach on the lines of IAS 16. Doing so may require an enterprise to segregate one asset into several parts, which may not be practicable in certain circumstances, at least at the beginning. It is therefore proposed that the components approach may be followed as an option until the industry is ready. ICAI also proposes to discuss the matter with the IASB to explore the possibility of providing guidance on the extent to which an asset can be divided into different components.

(ii) Accounting standard No. 15 – Employee Benefits (revised 2005):   In   respect   of termination benefits, the revised accounting standard No. 15 (2005), considering that industry in India is currently passing through a restructuring phase, specifically contains a transitional provision stating that – where an enterprise incurs expenditure on termination benefits on or before 31 March 2009 – it may choose to follow the accounting policy of deferring such expenditure over its pay-back period. However, expenditure so deferred cannot be carried forward to accounting periods commencing on or after 1 April 2010. IAS 19 does not provide such a transitional provision. These are given in India, in view of the interests of the industry at large.

(iii) Accounting standard No. 22 – Accounting for Taxes on Income: ICAI   issued accounting standard No. 22 in 2001 to introduce the international concept of deferred taxes in India for the first time. A number of companies challenged the standard in the courts, primarily because it affected their bottom line and the retained earnings particularly in the year in which the standard is introduced. It is an important lesson, as it is a new concept which has been met with widespread acceptance as companies are prepared to go to the courts to obtain relief; such standards should be therefore introduced gradually so that their impact may be softened. The legal cases pertaining to accounting standard No. 22 are still pending in the court.

(2) Lessons learned in addressing differences in the accounting treatment prescribed in IFRS and law: As a standard-setter, ICAI has learned a lesson that where the conceptually superior accounting treatments prescribed in various IFRS are in conflict with the corresponding legal requirements, there are various ways to deal with it, including the following:

(i) Change the accounting requirements as per the law: This approach has generally been followed in some of the earlier ICAI accounting standards. The disadvantage of this approach is that the correct accounting treatment does not even get recognized in the country. Furthermore, if this approach is followed it becomes difficult to persuade legal authorities to

change the law subsequently on the basis of the conceptually superior accounting treatment prescribed in an IFRS. Accordingly, this approach has not normally been followed in recent accounting standards and is followed sparingly when the legal position is so well-entrenched that giving a different accounting treatment in a standard is considered totally unacceptable. Increasingly, the approach proposed in the paragraph (ii) below is currently being adopted.

Where the accounting treatment is conceptually superior in an IFRS compared to the treatment prescribed in a law, the standard lays down the approach recommended by the IFRS, while recognizing that the law will prevail until a change is made in the relevant legal requirements. The advantage of this approach is that while the correct accounting treatment is recognized in an accounting standard in the country, it is also recognized that a change in law is imperative. For example, in the recently issued exposure draft of the proposed accounting standard on financial instruments (presentation), while the exposure draft recognizes that certain financial instruments such as preference shares should be classified as equities or liabilities depending upon their substance, it is also recognized that schedule VI to the Companies Act (1956), which lays down the presentation and disclosure requirements for the companies, and accordingly requires that the preference shares to be classified as equity, will have to be followed by the companies until it is amended.

(3) Guidance needs to be provided in various cases for effective implementation of accounting standards: Adequate guidance needs to be provided for effective implementation of accounting standards. In some cases, where accounting standards require management of the enterprises concerned to use judgement in making accounting estimates etc., various issues arise in the actual implementation. To address those issues, ICAI has issued accounting standards interpretations, guidance notes and other explanatory material. For example, accounting standard No. 16 on borrowing costs corresponding to IAS 23, defines the term "qualifying asset" as "an asset that necessarily takes a substantial period of time to get ready for its intended use or sale". The issue as to what constitutes "substantial period of time" has been addressed by issuance of accounting standard interpretation 1 on substantial period of time.

Furthermore, ICAI has also undertaken various projects for providing guidance on accounting matters arising from issuance of a new accounting standard, for example, it has recently undertaken to prepare a guide on estimating future cash flows and discount rates in the context of accounting standard No. 28 on impairment of assets.

(4) Capacity-building required before issuance of some of the newer accounting standards or revision of accounting standards corresponding to IFRS: Nowadays, with the issuance of newer accounting standards or revision of existing ones on the basis of IFRS, various new concepts are being introduced in India for which preparers and auditors need to be adequately trained; by organizing workshops, conducting seminars, etc. It is increasingly recognized that the preparers and auditors should be given training even before final issuance of a new standard, at the exposure draft stage itself, so that when the standard is finally issued, they are ready to effectively implement the standard.

V. Conclusion

Irrespective of various challenges, adoption of IFRS in India has significantly changed the contents of corporate financial statements as a result of:

– More refined measurements of performance and state of affairs, and

– Enhanced disclosures leading to greater transparency.

With the rapid liberalization process experienced in India over the past decade, there is now a huge presence of multinational enterprises in the country. Furthermore, Indian companies are also investing in foreign markets. This has generated an interest in Indian GAAP by all concerned. In this context, the role of Indian accounting standards, which are becoming closer to IFRS, has assumed a great significance from the point of view of global financial reporting.

Indian companies using the Indian accounting standards are experiencing fewer difficulties accessing international financial markets, as Indian accounting standards are becoming closer to IFRS. Indian standards are expected to converge even further in the future, especially after the challenges mentioned in study are addressed over the next few years.

Appendix A: Comparative statement of International Accounting Standards/international financial reporting standards and Indian accounting standards

(As on 8 June 2006)

I.   **Indian Accounting Standards already issued by the Institute of Chartered Accountants of India (ICAI) corresponding to the International Accounting Standards/international financial reporting standards**

No.	International Accounting Standards (IAS)/international financial reporting standards (IFRS)[42]		Indian accounting standards (AS)	
	No.	Title of the standard	AS No.	Title of the standard
1.	IAS 1	Presentation of Financial Statements	AS 1	Disclosure of Accounting Policies[43]
2.	IAS 2	Inventories	AS 2	Valuation of Inventories
3.		Corresponding IAS has been withdrawn since the matter is now covered by IAS 16 and IAS 38	AS 6	Depreciation Accounting[44]
4.	IAS 7	Cash Flow Statements	AS 3	Cash Flow Statements
5.	IAS 8	Accounting Policies, Changes in Accounting Estimates and Errors	AS 5	Net Profit or Loss for the Period, Prior Period Items and Changes in Accounting Policies[2]
6.	IAS 10	Events After the Balance Sheet Date	AS 4	Contingencies and Events Occurring after the Balance Sheet Date[2]
7.	IAS 11	Construction Contracts	AS 7	Construction Contracts
8.	IAS 12	Income Taxes	AS 22	Accounting for Taxes on Income
9.	IAS 14	Segment Reporting	AS 17	Segment Reporting
10.	IAS 16	Property, Plant and Equipment	AS 10	Accounting for Fixed Assets[2]
11.	IAS 17	Leases	AS 19	Leases
12.	IAS 18	Revenue	AS 9	Revenue Recognition[2]
13.	IAS 19	Employee Benefits	AS 15	Employee Benefits
14.	IAS 20	Accounting for Government Grants and Disclosure of Government Assistance	AS 12	Accounting for Government Grants[2]
15.	IAS 21	The Effects of Changes in Foreign Exchange Rates	AS 11	The Effects of Changes in Foreign Exchange Rates
16.	IAS 23	Borrowing Costs	AS 16	Borrowing Costs
17.	IAS 24	Related Party Disclosures	AS 18	Related Party Disclosures

[42] It may be noted that IAS Nos. 3, 4, 5, 6, 9, 13, 15, 22, 25, 30 and 35 have already been withdrawn by the International Accounting Standards Board (IASB).

[43] Under revision.

[44] It may be noted that accounting standard No. 10 on accounting for fixed assets is presently under revision to bring it in line with the corresponding IAS 16. After the issuance of the revised accounting standard No. 10, the withdrawal of accounting standard No. 6 has been proposed.

18.	IAS 27	Consolidated and Separate Financial Statements	AS 21	Consolidated Financial Statements
19.	IAS 28	Investments in Associates	AS 23	Accounting for Investments in Associates in Consolidated Financial Statements
20.	IAS 31	Interests in Joint Ventures	AS 27	Financial Reporting of Interests in Joint Ventures
21.	IAS 33	Earnings Per Share	AS 20	Earnings Per Share
22.	IAS 34	Interim Financial Reporting	AS 25	Interim Financial Reporting
23.	IAS 36	Impairment of Assets	AS 28	Impairment of Assets
24.	IAS 37	Provisions, Contingent Liabilities and Contingent Assets	AS 29	Provisions, Contingent Liabilities and Contingent Assets
25.	IAS 38	Intangible Assets	AS 26	Intangible Assets
26.		Corresponding IAS has been withdrawn since the matter is now covered by IAS 32, 39, 40 and IFRS 7	AS 13	Accounting for Investments[45]
27.	IAS 40	Investment Property	–	Dealt with by AS13[46]
28.	IFRS 3	Business Combinations	AS 14	Accounting for Amalgamations[47]
29.	IFRS 5	Non-current Assets Held for Sale and Discontinued Operations	AS 24	Discontinuing Operations.[48] Further, accounting standard No. 10 deals with accounting for fixed assets retired from active use.

II.   IAS/IFRS not considered relevant for issuance of accounting standards by ICAI and the reason.

No.	IAS/IFRS		
	No.	Title of the standard	Reasons
1.	IAS 29	Financial Reporting in Hyperinflationary Economies	ICAI notes that the hyperinflationary conditions do not prevail in India. Accordingly, the subject is not considered relevant in the Indian context.
2.	IFRS1	First-time Adoption of International Financial Reporting Standards	In India, Indian AS have been adopted over many years and IFRS are not being adopted for the first time. Therefore, IFRS 1 is not relevant to India at present.

---

[45] Indian accounting standard on financial instruments (recognition and measurement) is presently under preparation. After the issuance of this Indian AS, it is proposed that accounting standard No. 13 be withdrawn.

[46] Indian accounting standard corresponding to IAS 40 is also under preparation.

[47] Under revision.

[48] The IASB recently issued IFRS 5 and withdrew IAS 35 on discontinuing operations, on which accounting standard No. 24 is based. An Indian accounting standard corresponding to IFRS 5 is under preparation. After its issuance, it is proposed that accounting standard No. 24 be withdrawn.

III. **Accounting standards corresponding to the IAS/IFRS presently under preparation**

No.	IAS/IFRS		Status
	No.	Title of the standard	
1.	IAS 26	Accounting and Reporting by Retirement Benefit Plans	Under preparation.
2.	IAS 32	Financial Instruments: Presentation	Under preparation. Exposure draft issued.
3.	IAS 39	Financial Instruments: Recognition and Measurement	Under preparation.
4.	IAS 41	Agriculture	Under preparation.
5.	IFRS 2	Share-based Payment	Under preparation. At present, employee-share-based payments are covered by a guidance note issued by ICAI, which is based on IFRS 2. Furthermore, some other pronouncements deal with other share-based payments, e.g., accounting standard No. 10 on accounting for fixed assets.
6.	IFRS 4	Insurance Contracts	Under preparation.
7.	IFRS 7	Financial Instruments: Disclosures	Under preparation.

IV. **Guidance notes issued by ICAI corresponding to IAS/IFRS**

No	IAS/IFRS		Title of the guidance note
	No.	Title of the standard	
1.	IFRS 6	Exploration for and Evaluation of Mineral Resources	Guidance Note on Accounting for Oil and Gas-Producing Activities

Appendix B. Reconciliation of the International Accounting Standards/international financial reporting standards with the Indian accounting standards

(As on June 8, 2006)

(A) IAS/IFRS issued by the IASB

Number of IAS issued by the IASB	41
Number of IFRS issued by the IASB	7
Less: Number of IAS since withdrawn	(11)
Add: IAS 4 has been withdrawn, but, included here for reconciliation purposes because corresponding accounting standard of ICAI (i.e. accounting standard No. 6) is still in force	1
	38

(B) Accounting standards and other documents issued by ICAI

1.	Number of Indian accounting standards issued (excluding accounting standard No. 8 which is withdrawn pursuant to accounting standard No. 26 becoming mandatory)	28
2.	IAS/IFRS not relevant in the Indian context	2
3.	Guidance note issued by ICAI[49]	1
4.	Number of accounting standards under preparation	7
		38

---

[49] Corresponding to IFRS 6 (effective 2006) on exploration for and evaluation of mineral resources, ICAI guidance note entitled "Accounting for Oil and Gas-Producing Activities", has been issued.

Chapter V

Case study of Jamaica

I. Introduction[50]

For many years, Jamaican accounting standards comprised a mix of International Accounting Standards (IAS), IAS adapted to local peculiarities and locally developed standards to meet the needs of Jamaican companies. With the trend towards global harmonization of accounting standards, the International Accounting Standards Committee (IASC) issued a new directive that prohibited countries such as Jamaica from claiming to be in substantial compliance with IAS. This prompted Jamaica to reconsider its standard-setting practices.

Following the significant improvements IASC made to IAS by revising a number of them, strengthening the standard-setting process, reducing or eliminating alternative treatments and meeting the mandate of the International Organization of Securities Commissions (IOSCO), Jamaica joined its Caribbean partners and an increasing number of countries in reviewing its standard-setting practices and ensuring harmonization of its standards with IAS in all respects, except where comparable standards were not available.

Jamaica adopted international reporting standards and international standards on auditing (ISAs) with effect from 1 July 2002. All companies, listed and private, are therefore required to apply international financial reporting standards (IFRS) in the preparation of their financial statements and to have these statements audited in accordance with ISAs. Prior to 1 July 2002, Jamaican accounting standards and generally accepted auditing standards had been used.

The change has yielded significant improvements in the quality of financial reporting and the regulatory framework in Jamaica. The financial statements have become significantly more complex, but the strong majority position is that Jamaican companies' financial reports are more comparable and consistent with best practice.

The Institute of Chartered Accountants of Jamaica has been a forerunner in promoting regulatory effectiveness and compliance with laws and regulations. The institute provided important input and guidance in the preparation of the Companies Act (2004).

It sought and obtained the support of regulators, the business community and the Government in its efforts to raise the standard of accountability, quality of financial information and corporate transparency. Financial reports are now of international standard and the economic environment is more investor-friendly. The institute has responsibility for standard-setting and monitoring compliance with the standards.

---

[50] This chapter was prepared and edited by the UNCTAD secretariat with significant inputs from Dennis Brown, Institute of Chartered Accountants of Jamaica.

Rationale for adoption of IFRS

The adoption of IFRS signalled the integration of Jamaica into mainstream accounting practice and aimed to ensure that the country's reporting was on a par with global standards. As noted by Daley (2003),[51] the quest for organizational change, based on improved operational performance, is likely to be a key issue in financial markets following periods of distress and crisis. Standards must be relevant at all times to the environment. Where gaps exist, the value and impact of the standards are not maximized.[52]

II. Regulatory framework

Jamaican regulatory oversight has undergone significant changes, particularly in respect of the financial sector. The system has been reformed since the financial crisis of 1996–1997 and is governed by principles and guidelines. This is attributable to the strengthening of the institutional framework. The regulatory framework is also generally in line with international best practices and the oversight is effectively managed. The regulatory authorities actively monitor the system and implement further reforms as required. Regulatory capitalization limits have been established for most financial institutions to provide them with reasonable safeguards against abnormalities.

The financial system is, however, interrelated to what are described as conglomerate structures that consequently deepen the oversight requirements of the regulators. The relationship poses a regulatory risk because of the likelihood of connected lending, conflicts of interest, multiple gearing and contagion in the event of an entity failure. In recent years, there has been a rapid emergence of securities dealers in response to the regulatory improvements and other market developments. The vulnerability of the dealers to interest rate shocks was, however, highly evident in 2003/2004 when the Bank of Jamaica significantly increased nominal interest rate – a move that resulted in those institutions being visibly exposed to near insolvency. The regulators responded with decisive actions requiring increased capital, operational accountability and monitoring of these sector entities.

To sustain their relevance and effectiveness, the regulators have embarked on a programme to strengthen their capacity by focusing on areas of weakness, adopting best practices and building staffing resources. The strengthening of inter-agency cooperation is also an improvement in the regulatory framework although more is required in this area. Another area on which the agencies with oversight responsibilities have focused is regulatory convergence to reduce unevenness and minimize opportunities for regulatory arbitrage. The objective is to ensure a regulatory framework that unites with global standards and is capable of promoting and sustaining a competitive economic environment.

---

[51] J.A. Daley (2003). *The Adoption of International Accounting Standards (IAS) in Jamaica: Implication for Financial Stability*.

[52] IFRS are developed by the International Accounting Standard Board (IASB). Standards developed by the International Accounting Standards Committee (IASC) are referred to International Accounting Standards (IAS). The full set of standards IFRS and IAS, including the interpretations are generally referred to as IFRS.

The transition to a high-quality financial reporting system must be accompanied by the underpinnings of efficient regulations and supervision and the strengthening of institutional capacity of oversight authorities.

A substantial number of bodies with different regulatory power and functions make up the regulatory framework in Jamaica. These include the:

(a)   Bank of Jamaica;
(b)   Financial Services Commission;
(c)   Jamaica Deposit Insurance Corporation;
(d)   Financial Regulatory Council;
(e)   Public Accountancy Board;
(f)   Institute of Chartered Accountants of Jamaica;
(g)   Companies Office of Jamaica (formerly, the Registrar of Companies);
(h)   Fair Trading Commission;
(i)   Office of Utilities Regulation;
(j)   Bureau of Standards of Jamaica;
(k)   National Environmental Protection Authority;
(l)   Jamaica Intellectual Protection Authority;
(m)   Jamaica Stock Exchange.

The Bank of Jamaica, the Financial Services Commission, the Jamaica Deposit Insurance Corporation, the Financial Regulatory Council and the Jamaica Stock Exchange combine regulatory functions for the financial services in Jamaica. The Public Accountancy Board, under the Ministry of Finance, and the Institute of Chartered Accountants of Jamaica share responsibility for the accountancy profession. Such responsibility entails admission, training, continuing education, monitoring of and compliance with professional standards and complaints and disciplinary issues.

Companies Act (2004)

All businesses and professionals, local and foreign, operating in Jamaica must adhere to its laws and regulations. The Companies Act (2004) is the primary source of legal requirements regarding the operation of a company, including corporate disclosures. The Companies Act (2004) is an act of Parliament that became effective 1 February 2005. It succeeded the Companies Act (1965), which was broadly based on the United Kingdom Companies Act of 1948. The new Act prescribes the basis for incorporation, regulation and winding-up of companies and other associations registered thereunder and makes provisions for other matters relating thereto. There are approximately 40,000 active companies registered under the Companies Act. Forty-two of these companies are publicly listed on the Jamaica Stock Exchange.

The Companies Act requires considerable disclosure and compliance and provides for increased penalties for failure to comply. The Act addresses disclosure and other regulatory requirements in relation to:

- Incorporation and registration;
- Disclosures to be made in a prospectus;
- Capitalization minimums;
- Management and administration;
- Duties and responsibilities of directors and other officers;
- Matters relating to winding-up;

- Registration and inspections;
- Accounts and audit;
- Annual reports; and
- Meetings and statutory filings.

The Companies Act specifically requires all registered companies to present financial statements in accordance with generally accepted accounting principles promulgated by the Institute of Chartered Accountants of Jamaica. The institute promulgates IFRS as the national accounting standards since 2002. The Act defines the content and form of the financial statements and requires companies to maintain proper accounting records and documents to show a true and fair view of the company's affairs and explain its transactions. In the case of group companies, the Act provides that consolidated financial statements must be presented, except where the company is a wholly owned subsidiary of another company incorporated in Jamaica. The contents of a set of financial statements as defined as:

(a) A balance sheet;
(b) Statement of changes in equity;
(c) A profit and loss account;
(d) Statement of changes in financial position; and
(e) Notes to the financial statements.

The legal requirement for companies to prepare IFRS-compliant financial statements facilitates an effective financial reporting system, as all companies are required to be in compliance. The institute has a regulatory mandate to set accounting and auditing standards. It has, however, no jurisdiction to ensure compliance by non-members. The following organizations are key agents in support of the regulatory framework and entities regulated by them are therefore required to comply.

Bank of Jamaica

The Bank of Jamaica is established by the Bank of Jamaica Act (1960) and began operations in 1961 to formulate and implement monetary and regulatory policies to safeguard the value of the domestic currency and to ensure the soundness of the financial system. Under the Bank of Jamaica Act, the Bank of Jamaica legally has supervisory oversight over institutions governed by the following pieces of legislation:

(a) Commercial banks governed by the Banking Act;
(b) Near-bank deposit-taking intermediaries, such as merchant banks, trust companies and financial houses licensed under the Financial Institutions Act;
(c) Building societies and institutions operating under the Industrial and Provident Societies Act that either take deposits and/or make loans.

The key regulatory provisions are contained in the Banking Act, the Financial Institutions Act, the Building Societies Act and the Bank of Jamaica (Building Societies) Regulations of 1995 that govern the licensing and "fit and proper" assessment in relation to shareholders, directors and management.

The regulatory provisions include:

- Regulations of shareholding in licences
- Minimum capital requirement

- Compulsory creation of reserves and profits
- Adequacy of capital
- Credit exposure limit
- Investment and fixed assets limits
- Cash reserves and liquidity assets
- Loan classification and provisioning guidelines
- Prudential returns and publication of accounts
- Appointment of auditors and
- Examination and sanctions.

Financial Services Commission

The Financial Services Commission derives its legal jurisdiction from the Securities Act that came into effect in 1993 to make provisions for the securities industry. The commission was established in 2001 to regulate and supervise all financial services that do not involve the taking of deposits, in accordance with the Financial Securities Act 2001 under which it was created. This regulatory body is commissioned to protect users of financial services in the areas of insurance, securities and pension by fostering the integrity, stability and health of the financial sector.

The commission administers the operations and activities of securities dealers, investment advisors, mutual funds, unit trusts, insurance companies, insurance brokers and agencies. Its mandate includes oversight of the registration, solvency and conduct of approximately 180 firms and 1,400 individuals. In doing so:

- It ensures compliance with the provisions of the Securities Act within the securities industry;
- It issues or refuses licences or registration upon application and suspends or cancels such licences or registration if so granted;
- It ensures compliance with the Insurance Act, the Financial Services Act and the Securities Act and regulates private persons.

Specific regulations exist that govern the criteria for licensing and registration of securities dealers, investment advisors and their representatives. It is illegal to conduct business in Jamaica without the requisite licence under the Act.

The commission implements its activities by administrating a number of laws, including the Insurance Act and regulations, the Financial Services Act, the Pensions Act, the Securities Act and the Unit Trusts Act. It addresses solvency standards and actuarial guidelines, appointed actuary, market and conduct standards, fitness and propriety, corporate governance and sanctions and penalties for non-compliance.

Under the Securities Act and regulations, the Commission covers areas of corporate governance, responsible official, fitness and propriety, mutual funds, issuer registration and capital requirements. The Unit Trusts Act may be substituted for mutual fund legislation to be enacted in the near future: it provides for fitness and proprietary and corporate governance requirements.

It is expected that, as part of the strengthening of the regulatory infrastructures, there will be clear distinction between the regulation and supervision of deposit-takers and the regulation and supervision of other financial services. This is necessary to diminish areas of regulatory unevenness that currently provide opportunity for regulatory arbitrage.

Financial Regulatory Council

The Financial Regulatory Council was established and commenced meeting in 2000. It is a policy-setting body established to facilitate convergence between the regulators and address evident unevenness of supervision, particularly between banking and other supervisors. Its aim is to ensure greater cohesiveness and efficiency of the financial system, as well as to eliminate regulatory gaps and arbitrage opportunities that can undermine financial stability. The Financial Regulatory Council is chaired by the Governor of the Bank of Jamaica. Other members include heads of the Financial Services Commission and the Jamaica Deposit Insurance Corporation and the Financial Secretary of the Ministry of Finance.

The council exercises its regulatory influence by sharing information – especially on dually supervised entities and groups such as conglomerates – critically identifying supervisory gaps and coordinating responses to problems discovered in the financial system. It also has a mandate to promote harmonization of prudential norms and the underlying principle of safety and soundness regardless of the complexity, range and diversity of financial groups and products.

Jamaica Deposit Insurance Corporation

The source of the Jamaica Deposit Insurance Corporation's authority is the Deposit Insurance Act of 1998. Its legislated mandate is to provide protection to small savers and exercises a shared role in safeguarding the country's financial system. Its key functions are to establish and manage a scheme for insurance of deposits against loss. The Deposit Insurance Act prescribes an insurance-cover limit for each depositor and provides for the establishment of a deposit insurance fund from which depositors will be paid if a financial institution fails to do so because of regulatory intervention by the Bank of Jamaica or the Minister of Finance.

The corporation does not have regulatory or supervisory authority. It must therefore work closely with the Bank of Jamaica to discharge its responsibilities effectively. The corporation is entitled to request and receive on-site reports and other relevant information from the Bank of Jamaica. Arrangements for information sharing between the bank and corporation are specified in the Deposit Insurance Act, although no such arrangements exist between the corporation and international agencies. The corporation's policy is to consult with the insured financial institutions before introducing mandates of a substantial technical nature. The board of directors and employees of this institution are bound by the provisions of the Public Bodies Management and Accountability Act.

The Act was established in 2001 and modified 2003 to address the operations of government-owned companies and statutory bodies. It seeks to increase the accountability of all public bodies and provides for, inter alia:

(a)   Improvements in corporate governance and accountability in reporting;
(b)   Establishment of a measure of duty of care, disclosure and general conduct of director and others;
(c)   Sanctions for non-compliance with the provisions relating to corporate governance and accountability; and
(d)   Detailing of the format and contents of reports to be generated by public entities.

In 2005, the Ministry of Finance set out, through its strategic programme, to achieve the effective regulation of financial institutions. It noted that continued stability in the financial sector is critical to the growth prospects of the country and, in this regard, reaffirms its intention through the Bank of Jamaica, the Financial Services Commission and the corporation to continue to employ strategies to maintain this stability. Specific focus is on:

(a)   Expediting the development of an adequate regulatory framework for private pensions;

(b)   Reducing money-laundering activities through improved legislation and closer partnership with international bodies;

(c)   Reinforcing the role of the regulatory agencies in the financial sector; and

(d)   Continuing institutional strengthening of the regulatory bodies.

The Ministry of Finance also recognizes the need to strengthen the financial management process of public entities by ensuring timely financial reporting and is working to that effect.

Public Accountancy Board

The Public Accountancy Act of 1968 established a regulatory framework for the accounting profession. The Act created the Public Accountancy Board, a statutory body, to issue licences to registered public accountants and promote acceptance standards of professional conduct by registered public accountants. Decisions by this regulatory agency are subject to approval by the Minister of Finance, who has authority to issue regulations relating to the profession. The minister's has the authority to, inter alia, make complaints against registered public accountants and regulations governing the disciplinary investigations undertaken by the Board and institute the procedure for approving applications for registration as a registered public accountant.

The board exercises its mandate as the legal authority that issues licences to registered public accountants (who must also hold a practising certificate from the board). Only registered public accountants have the legal authority to sign audit reports on financial statements. Practicing certificates may be issued to:

(a)   Members of the Institute of Chartered Accountants of Jamaica who hold practicing certificates from the institute;

(b)   Jamaican citizens who are entitled to practice in another country by virtue of another professional qualification appraised by the Minister of Finance; and

(c)   A few persons who are qualified by experience and who practised as public accountants prior to 1968.

The Institute of Chartered Accountants of Jamaica

The Institute of Charted Accountants was established in 1965 to regulate chartered accountants in Jamaica. It is responsible for setting accounting and auditing standards. Some of the broad objectives of the institute are to:

(a)   Promote and increase professional knowledge through training;

(b)   Regulate the discipline and professional conduct of Jamaican accountants; and

(c)   Develop and set standards to ensure the integrity and soundness of the accountancy profession.

The institute has approximately 800 members, of which 200 are practicing members, authorized by it to carry out audits. Members authorized by the institute to practice are entitled to practising certificates from the Public Accounting Board. There is no requirement for all registered public accountants or accountants in general to become members of the institute. Four major international professional services firms are represented in Jamaica, and three of the four audit virtually all listed companies operating in the country.

The Public Accountancy Board and the institute entered into an agreement to share the responsibility for ensuring unified standards for the control, monitoring and discipline of all registered public accountants in Jamaica and improving the effectiveness of the board as the legal authority for the oversight of registered practicing accountants in Jamaica. The financial services regulators rely significantly on external auditors of the regulated entities to ensure compliance with accounting and financial reporting requirements and report compliance failures. These firms are the primary source of knowledge on IFRS and ISA issues and share this knowledge routinely with the regulators, as these regulators are still in the process of strengthening the standards and procedures and building capacity to monitor and enforce compliance.

Currently, financial reporting compliance is monitored by reviewing published financial statements of all publicly listed companies and regulated entities. With the support of the Inter-American Development Bank under a cooperation agreement, the institute is in the process of establishing a more comprehensive monitoring and compliance programme. This programme will include peer reviews of auditing firms, practice-management reviews and identification of resource gaps.

The Institute is also collaborating with The Institute of Chartered Accountants of the Caribbean (ICAC) to establish a regional monitoring unit with responsibility for the evaluation and assessment of the quality of audit and other public practice work in member countries. The implementation of this unit will ensure transparency of the quality of audits and other public practice work. The arrangement with the ICAC is intended to facilitate independence in the practice monitoring process.

The institute is a member of International Federation of Accountants (IFAC) and requires its members to comply with IFAC ethical, professional and educational standards. The standards issued by the institute include both the standards issued by IFAC and those promulgated by the institute. Professional education requirements for becoming a member of the institute are consistent with international standards and must meet continuing professional development requirements of at least 35 hours of qualifying professional education annually, over three years. So that members can meet to this requirement, the institute hosts a number of educational training programmes, which are also promoted to the wider community.

Companies Office of Jamaica (formerly, Office of the Registrar of Companies)

The Companies Office of Jamaica falls under the Ministry of Industry, Commerce and Technology and is responsible for the day-to-day administration of companies, trademarks, industrial designs, industrial and provident societies, business names and recording of patents.

The office registers local and overseas companies, industrial and provident societies and individuals carrying out business in Jamaica. Its mandate is to ensure that there is compliance with the Companies Act, the Registration of Business Names Act and the Industrial and Provident Societies Act. It also maintains up-to-date records of all companies and businesses registered.

All companies registered under the Companies Act must file prescribed returns, including annual returns, with the Companies Office of Jamaica. This agency is empowered to take legal action against delinquent entities to enforce compliance.

Jamaica Stock Exchange

The Jamaica Stock Exchange was established as a private limited-liability company in August 1968 and commenced trading in February 1969. Its primary objectives are to:

- Promote the development of the stock market in Jamaica;
- Ensure the stock market and participants operate at the highest standard;
- Develop and enforce rules designed to ensure public confidence in the market;
- Provide facilities for the trade of stock; and
- Conduct research and provide information to and on the market.

The company has a board of 18 directors and facilitates trade in securities, shares, ordinary and preference and corporate bonds. Government bonds are not listed on the Jamaica Stock Exchange, but by the Bank of Jamaica on an over-the-counter market. Listing of securities on the Jamaica Stock Exchange is, however, at the absolute discretion of its council. The minimum requirements for listing of a company's securities are:

- Total issued share and loan capital of $500,000 or more
- Minimum number of 100 shareholders for companies with ordinary shares.

Companies established in Jamaica may be listed by a prospectus issue, an offer for sale, an offer by tender, a placing or an introduction. In 2000, the Jamaica Stock Exchange established the Jamaica Central Securities Depository. As a result of this development, share certificates are dematerialized. There has been increased global attractiveness of the stock market because of the adoption of generally accepted international standards.

Financial reporting and disclosure

Jamaica has a differential disclosure regime for financial reporting purposes. The types of companies may be classified as:

(a)   Publicly listed and regulated companies;
(b)   Private companies; and
(c)   Small companies.

All companies are required to prepare annual financial statements. These statements must be audited and circulated to the members, except for small companies that may claim exemption under the Companies Act. Companies are also required to file annually a true copy of the balance sheet and profit and loss account and a copy of the auditors' report with the Companies Office of Jamaica.

In addition to meeting the disclosure requirements, publicly listed companies are required to file with the Jamaica Stock Exchange and publish in the media quarterly, abridged financial statements. These must be accompanied by a directors' report and signed by at least two directors.

Companies file their annual financial statements within 90 days of the end of their financial year and quarterly financial statements within 45 days of the end of the quarter. Qualifying small companies may seek exemption under the Companies Act from audit of its financial statements and from preparing the financial statements to comply with IFRS.

There are three important aspects of the Jamaican financial reporting framework that should be noted:

(a)   IFRS must be used by all entities in their preparation of financial statements. Qualifying small companies that elect exemption from preparing these financial statements and accordingly may omit to do so, but must apply the standards issued by the Institute of Chartered Accountants of Jamaica that are applicable to their nature and complexity to show a true and fair view of their state of affairs and results of operations;

(b)   International Standards on Auditing (ISAs) to audit financial statements;

(c)   Monitoring of the system to ensure there is compliance with the Companies Act and IFRS in the preparation of financial statements and that the financial statements are audited in accordance with ISAs.

III. Capacity-building

One of the challenges confronting a developing country such as Jamaica is the creation of a sustainable economic environment that promotes adequate corporate disclosure and is supported by an effective legal and regulatory infrastructure. The benefits of underpinning the country's financial reporting system with a set of high-quality globally recognized financial reporting standards are considered significant in achieving this end.

Reporting under IFRS gives rise to expected outcomes of clarity, comparability and consistency, which are important elements for an investor in assessing a country's attractiveness. It was important therefore for Jamaica to build the capacity to sustain an improved financial reporting framework as bolstered by an efficient and responsive legal and regulatory infrastructure. Some key elements that have been identified as critical underpinnings for the sustainability of this framework are:

- Professional education and training
- Sound corporate disclosure to be achieved through an effective process of dissemination of corporate reports
- Allocation of resources and
- Efficient monitoring and compliance.

The anticipated results from the implementation of these elements were:

- Stimulation of a system of broader conformity
- Improved investor confidence
- General public esteem and
- Enhancement of the profession's reputation.

As a key driver in this process of change to an enabling environment of legal and regulatory frameworks, the Institute of Chartered Accountants of Jamaica identified a number of challenges that require specific action as part of this process of strengthening institutional and human resource capabilities and contributing to a wider system of capacity-building.

The capacity-building agents identified are the:

- Regulators: These agencies were created and empowered by specific laws and regulations to issue mandates and enforce compliance. Therefore, efficiency and effectiveness of the regulatory framework is influenced by how well regulatory agencies perform.

- Investors: Investors benefit when financial statements, accounting standards and auditing procedures are prepared on a consistent basis and are comparable across industries and countries. Investors must be empowered with adequate knowledge to be able to interpret the financial statements and understand the basis for fluctuations and swings in the performance of companies and the market.

- Government ministries: The Government sets macroeconomic policies that influence economic growth and national focus. The Government is also responsible for enacting laws establishing the legal system. The Government's understanding of the relationship between an effective legal and regulatory system and economic growth is an important factor in capacity-building.

- Accountancy profession: The critical capacity-building agent in the successful implementation of IFRS in Jamaica is the Institute of Chartered Accountants of Jamaica. The accountancy profession, represented by its institute, masterminded and championed the transition to IFRS to enhance the financial reporting system. The transition entails peer-to-peer learning, institutional development, training, research and publishing.

- Stakeholders (financial analysts and other users): Financial analysts are expected to be able to assess the quality of a company's reported performance and evaluate the appropriateness of management's forecasts. Similarly, other users should have the competence to understand the company's business and whether the business model is consistent with reported results. The stakeholders include other sectoral interest groups, including academics.

Four key focus areas adopted as part of the programme of transition included:

- Training
- Human resource development – equipping individuals with increased knowledge, information and training to ensure they are able to perform at a higher standard
- Organizational development – providing guidance in how to improve processes and structures to effectively apply the provisions of the new standards
- Institutional and regulatory framework – enhancing the resource capability of the institute as a source of reference, collaborating with regulations by inviting their participation in committee discussions and assisting them with training; also, contributing to debates on legal and regulatory changes.

Some specific areas undertaken as part of the process to ensure the successful and sustainable effectiveness of the new reporting framework are as follows:

(a) *Building expertise and professional capacity within the accountancy profession.* This has been achieved through increased training, improved access to by-laws and accounting principles, and a programme of improved collaboration and cooperation with regulators, particularly within the financial sector. Increased collaboration was also forged with professional and trade associations.

(b) *Strengthening the institute's oversight capabilities.* The key was to establish expert committees on each major sectoral interest, including taxation, accounting and auditing, banking and other activities addressed under the Banking Act, and near-bank and related activities covered under the Financial Institutions Act and the Insurance Act. Committee members were intensely trained in the relevant subject area to provide the appropriate guidance. In addition, the aim has been to strengthen the investigative and disciplinary capabilities of the institute to provide effective oversight of delinquent members and to be able to identify and report breaches of non-members, as appropriate. Significant improvements have been made by the regulators in enhancing their capacity to provide effective oversight over their sectoral areas. Laws have introduced or strengthened to increase the penalties for violations. The programme also included the creation of a resource/research centre as an information source to members of the institute and the wider community.

(c) *Assisting in strengthening the legal framework.* Efforts continue to be made to encourage the establishment of a regional monitoring unit to promote individual and firm-wide compliance with the standards. The institute has been working with the relevant bodies to overcome the legal restrictions in some regional territories. The desire is to have a single regional monitoring unit that covers the eight major English-speaking countries of the region.

(d) *Collaborating with trade associations and regulators to promote good governance practices.* The decision to adopt IFRS and ISAs as the respective national accounting and auditing standards was deemed an important step in enhancing the financial reporting capacity. It was however, also important to ensure that this capacity was further strengthened by rigorous interpretation and application of the standards on a country-wide basis. In this regard, the institute entered into a technical cooperation agreement with Inter-American Development Bank for funding assistance. The broad areas of the agreement are:

- The dissemination of information on IFRS
- Training and outreach
- Building enforcement and compliance capabilities of IFRS
- Building sustainable training programmes.

Following the Institute's decision to make the transition to IFRS, the World Bank sponsored an assessment of the implementation of accounting and auditing standards as part of a programme to determine the gaps in standards and compliance. The review was undertaken as part of the Reports on the Observance of Standards and Codes initiative.

Utilizing the results of that review and recognizing that elements of the gaps identified were due to human and institutional resource constraints, the institute committed itself to building financial resources to ensure its capacity-building efforts would be sustained.

(e) *Developing a country action plan, setting out a logistic framework of targeted activities to be completed within a specified period.* This included having road shows to explain the objective, consequences and benefits of the change to global standards and the need for compliance, raising government ministers' awareness of the potential impact of the conversion to IFRS, including the benefits and regulatory synergies to be derived, meeting with business leaders and giving them guidance on communicating the impact of the change on business performance and the market as a whole, including the need to review the effects on agreement covenants. Auditing firms were also involved as channels for communicating to and assisting with the training programme, including specific training for their clients.

(f) *Designing and implementing a task-driven action programme.* The programme elements include:

- The Consultative Committee including sectoral experts to be fully functional to assist on an ongoing basis;

- A strategic publicity and educational programme that routinely addresses important IFRS and ISA issues in the media, on the institute's website and in specially arranged seminars and workshops;

- Strategic seminars and workshops conducted by internationally recognized experts to train users and preparers of financial statements, develop ability to interpret and apply the standards;

- Development of a programme to review of financial statements and communicate significant findings to the lead engagement auditors;

- "Train the trainer" sessions utilizing international experts to build a pool of specialized local trainers to ensure sustainability of high-quality trainers;

- Efforts to make into law the requirement to prepare financial statements using IFRS. This is being achieved by participating in special review of Companies Act 2004 whose purpose is to include this requirement;

- Reliance on auditing firms to build and utilize their training skills and competence to assist in building stakeholders' awareness. This provision also includes hosting training sessions for their clients and providing them with helpful toolkits to guide them in the conversion process;

- Strengthening of the institute's by-laws and disciplinary committees to ensure sanctions are applied for major violations; and

- Identification of a set of standards applicable to small entities and their adoption as the small company standards. Currently, these companies need to apply IFRS under the Companies Act.

IV. Lessons learned

The creation of an enabling environment that is bolstered by an effective regulatory framework is an important factor in the economic development of a country. To ensure investor attractiveness, such an economy must have a strong financial reporting framework as evidenced by high-quality global standards.

The adoption of IFRS in 2002 helped to strengthen Jamaican financial systems by encouraging stronger regulation and supervision, greater transparency and more efficient and robust institutions, markets and infrastructure. It also represents a major change in the country's reporting structure.

The ethos of IFRS is fair value accounting and that presents interpretational and application challenges for most stakeholders. The underlying emphasis of this concept is the recognition of the substance of a transaction over its form. The potential vulnerability in reported results arising from fluctuations in the value of assets and liabilities was consistently illuminated in discussions with market players. There are underlying fears that must be overcome. Many of those involved deemed IFRS as more relevant to multinational corporations and, in most instances, inappropriate to such smaller entities as exist in developing economies like Jamaica. Nevertheless, the expected benefits – which include increased financial stability, better investment and lending decisions, informed market integrity and reduced risk of financial distress and contagion – outweigh the disadvantages.

Some key lessons learned from exercise are:

(a) Effective implementation of IFRS requires careful planning and extensive public education, the allocation of resources, a legal and regulatory support system and institutional support with strong management systems. Unless stakeholders are involved and included in development plans and how they are affected, they will be reluctant to support the change.

(b) The communications system for informing users of the changes in reporting requirements must be effective and responsive. Users of financial statements have to be able to interpret financial reports and raise questions about an entity's performance. Efforts to build good corporate governance and enhance corporate transparency will be successful only when these key stakeholders have the desired knowledge to understand the financial reports and interrogate reported information.

(c) Adequate resources must be put in place to support the sustainable implementation of IFRS and ISAs. This includes having consultative groups available to respond promptly to concerns by users and to provide for their ongoing training. Assisting key stakeholders, including regulators with training to ensure they have the required resources to interpret and apply the requirements of IFRS, is a critical element in the successful implementation of IFRS.

(d) Many of the standards include complex and detailed disclosure issues applicable to larger companies. However, as the majority of companies in Jamaica are small or medium-sized enterprises, alternatives have to be put in place to accommodate their needs. Suitable standards must, therefore, be developed to facilitate recognition of these companies.

(e) Continuing training is an important factor in transitioning to IFRS. The continuous and wide-scale changes present a significant challenge for a developing country with limited resources and available experts. It is, however, important to ensure that training is available for auditors, regulators, analysts and other users necessary.

(f) A strong institutional framework must be in place to champion and manage the change process.

(g) The adoption of IFRS can have an impact on the country's national statistics. Data on productivity, efficiency and profitability are often collected by the government statistical authority for national reporting.

Chapter VI

Case study of Kenya

I. Introduction and background[53]

This case study focuses on Kenya, which was one of the first countries to adopt the use of international financial reporting standards (IFRS) and International Accounting Standards (IAS) in 1999. Over the years, Kenya has developed a wealth of experience in the use of IFRS which would provide useful insights in the development of strategies by ISAR to aid other countries in the implementation of IFRS.

There is one stock market in Kenya, the Nairobi Stock Exchange, in which the shares of about 50 companies are traded. In addition to these listed companies, there is also a sizeable number of companies which are either multinationals or owned privately by Kenyans, as well as a large number of small and medium-sized enterprises (SMEs). In terms of financial reporting, all these companies are required to prepare financial statements based on IFRS. In most cases, however, most SMEs would prepare financial statements for use by the tax authorities or by the banks for purposes of accessing credit.

Other public interest companies such as banks, insurance companies, cooperative societies and non-governmental organizations also prepare accounts in accordance with IFRS.

With respect to auditing, all companies are required to be audited in accordance with the international standards on auditing (ISAs). In most cases, though, it is the larger companies that seek to be audited. SMEs are only audited when necessary for tax purposes or as a requirement to access credit. The auditing sector/industry in Kenya is fragmented, with about 500 practising firms. Of these, four are considered as large and with international linkages and they audit practically all the large multinationals, banks, insurance companies and the listed companies. There are about 10 medium-sized firms with more than two partners, and the rest of the audit firms are largely one or two-partner firms.

---

[53] This document was prepared and edited by the UNCTAD secretariat with substantive inputs from Caroline J. Kigen, Institute of Certified Public Accountants of Kenya.

II. Regulatory framework governing financial reporting in Kenya

Statutory framework governing the accountancy profession in Kenya

The accounting profession in Kenya is regulated by the Accountants Act, which was enacted on 1 July 1977. The Accountants Act established three bodies, namely the:

(a) Kenya Accountants and Secretaries National Examinations Board (KASNEB), which was given the responsibility of administering examinations for persons wishing to qualify for registration as accountants and company secretaries. KASNEB administers the examinations for accounting technicians and the higher-level certified public accountants examinations.

(b) Registration of Accountants Board, which was charged with registering candidates who have attained the specified qualifications after passing the relevant examinations administered by KASNEB. Persons holding designated foreign accountancy qualifications can be registered with the board after passing the examinations in company law and taxation administered by KASNEB. The board also issues practising certificates to those who have met the requirements prescribed for issuance of a practising certificate. These requirements include prior registration and membership of the Institute of Certified Public Accountants of Kenya as an accountant, as well as relevant experience in auditing for a minimum period of two years.

(c) Institute of Certified Public Accountants of Kenya (ICPAK), which is responsible for the oversight of the profession. Once a person is registered as an accountant by the Registration of Accountants Board, he or she becomes eligible for membership of ICPAK. ICPAK is mandated by the Accountants Act to:

> (i) Promote standards of professional competence and practice amongst members of the institute;
> (ii) Promote research into accountancy, finance and related matters, and the publication of books, periodicals, journals and articles in connection therewith;
> (iii) Promote the international recognition of the institute;
> (iv) Advise the Examinations Board on matters relating to examination standards and policies;
> (v) Carry out any other functions prescribed for it under any of the other provisions of this Act or under any other written law; and
> (vi) Do anything incidental or conducive to the performance of any of the preceding functions.

Membership of ICPAK is voluntary. Currently, there are around 3,500 members of ICPAK, whereas statistics available from KASNEB indicate that, as at the end of 2005, there were a total of 10,500 persons who had completed the final level of certified public accountants examinations.

The existing statutory framework described above provides for the regulation of the profession through three separate entities. This poses various challenges, particularly with regard to decisions that impact the whole spectrum of accounting profession. ICPAK is a member of the

International Federation of Accountants (IFAC) and is responsible for the implementation of international education standards aimed at strengthening the public-accountant certification process; the process is, however, managed by KASNEB. There is a need for the two institutions to work closely together and the need for consensus-building obviously means that there will be delays in undertaking any reforms related to the process. There are also challenges in coordinating the work of ICPAK and Registration of Accountants Board to ensure that quality standards are observed.

With respect to financial reporting and auditing, the Accountants Act does not explicitly state that ICPAK has the authority to issue standards of professional practice, including accounting and auditing standards which shall form the basis of accountancy practice in the preparation, verification and auditing of financial statements. Although financial statements are currently prepared in accordance with standards prescribed by ICPAK, there are currently no legal requirements for companies to comply with the standards issued by ICPAK.

The weaknesses in the Accountants Act are being addressed through a revision of the Act that is being undertaken by a taskforce appointed by the Minister of Finance in 2004. The proposed changes that will impact on financial reporting include giving ICPAK the legal authority to issue standards for use in financial reporting and auditing.

Statutory framework governing financial reporting in Kenya

In Kenya, the main legislation governing companies, including financial reporting, is the Companies Act. However, there are other laws that have an incidence on financial reporting. These deal with specialized sectors such as the insurance sector, banks and listed companies.

Companies Act (CAP 486)

The Companies Act requires all limited liability companies to prepare and keep proper books of accounts as are necessary to give a true and fair view of the state of the companies' affairs and to explain its transactions. The Act further requires companies to present a profit and loss account and a balance sheet each year during its annual general meeting and prescribes in detail what should be included in the profit and loss account and the balance sheet.

The Kenyan Companies Act, borrowed from the Companies Act of 1948 of the United Kingdom, does not reflect the requirements set out in the Accountants Act and neither does it recognize ICPAK's authority to oversee and prescribe the financial reporting framework to be adhered to by companies in preparing financial statements. The "true and fair view" concept is not defined in the Act.

The Companies Act prescribes in detail what should be included in financial reports but some of the requirements of the Act fall short of those of IFRS. For example, the Act does not require preparation of a cash flow statement.

With respect to audits, the Act requires companies to appoint auditors who must be members of the Institute and who meet the criteria for an auditor as laid out in the Accountants Act. The Act further specifies that the auditors' report should appear as an annex to the profit and loss account and balance sheet and prescribes the contents of the auditors' report. However, the Act does not specifically require the auditor to conduct audits in accordance with ISAs.

Industry-specific legislation governing financial reporting

Various industries are governed by specialized laws, which make provisions with regard to financial reporting. Some of the legislation requires the use IFRS and ISAs as the basis for preparation and auditing of financial statements, including regulations issued by the Capital Markets Authority, governing the companies whose shares are listed and traded on the Nairobi Stock Exchange, and regulations issued by the Central Bank of Kenya governing banks operating in Kenya. Thus, listed companies and banks are specifically required to use IFRS in the preparation and audit of their financial statements.

In the case of the insurance sector in Kenya, while the Insurance Act requires preparation and audit of accounts, the Act does not specify the basis for preparing these accounts. The Act further specifies various schedules that must be filled in by the companies containing prescribed financial information. These should be sent to the commissioner of insurance annually. With the issue of IFRS 4 on insurance contracts, it emerged that the provisions of the schedules as contained in the Act were contrary to the provisions of the standard. Conflicts emerged regarding how insurance companies would prepare their financial statements and, after extensive discussions between ICPAK and the Commissioner of Insurance in Kenya, it was agreed that companies would prepare one set of financial statements that are IFRS-compliant and would also fill in the schedules as provided in the Act and send them to the Commissioner of Insurance. However, where the figures in the schedules prescribed by the insurance act differed from those in the financial statements that are prepared in accordance with IFRS, then companies were to prepare appropriate reconciliations which were to be certified by the auditor. This of course places a burden on insurance companies in Kenya.

Other regulations affecting on financial reporting include legislation dealing with retirement benefit schemes, cooperative societies and local authorities. In some cases the provisions of these laws hinder the implementation of IFRS.

To deal with these regulatory challenges, ICPAK has adopted a policy of working with various regulators to raise their awareness of the importance and need for IFRS and, ultimately, to promote ICPAK's role as the authority governing financial reporting. ICPAK continues to lobby for the incorporation of IFRS as the reporting framework in various laws governing financial reporting in Kenya. In this regard, ICPAK recognizes that regulators may not have the technical expertise on financial reporting aspects and therefore works with them in revising legal provisions to align them with IFRS provisions.

III. Implementation status: accounting and auditing standards

In 1998, the ICPAK council made the historic decision to adopt international financial reporting and auditing standards for use in Kenya. Accordingly, all companies were required to prepare financial statements based on International Accounting Standards (IAS) for periods beginning 1 January 1999, while the audits of all financial statements for period ending 31 December 1999 were to be carried out according to ISAs.

Prior to those dates, ICPAK had issued Kenyan accounting and auditing standards that were largely modified from the IAS and ISAs to suit the Kenyan environment. The decision to adopt international reporting standards fully was made at a time when the Kenyan business scene was reeling from numerous bank failures in the 1980s and 1990s. These failures raised questions as to the reliability of audited financial information, in particular, because the financial statements of these banks did not provide any early warning signs of their failures.

The 1990s were also characterized by privatization of companies that were previously wholly State-owned. Some of the privatization was through a sale of shares on the Nairobi Stock Exchange. Interest in the capital markets was beginning and, to sustain this interest, there was a need to improve corporate governance practices that prevailed at the time.

ICPAK recognized that, to promote confidence in the capital markets and in the business environment in general, the country needed a globally accepted reporting framework which would result in quality financial reporting and address the expectation of the users of financial statements. Indeed, at this time there was pressure from various regulators including those charged with overseeing the capital markets and the Central Bank to adopt IAS, as these reflected best global practice.

The ICPAK council also took into account the scarce resources available at ICPAK. Rather than utilize these scarce resources in the development of standards, it was felt that it would be more useful to utilize these resources to interpret IAS and provide user support. In any event, most of the Kenyan standards that had been issued to date were to a large extent compliant with international standards, albeit with a few modifications. During this period, there were 18 Kenyan accounting standards and about 20 Kenyan auditing guidelines in use. At the time of adopting international standards, standards included IAS 1–39 and ISAs 100–930 and international auditing practice statements Nos. 100–1011. Of the Kenyan accounting standards, six of them had no material differences with the corresponding IAS, while the others had a few differences. About 20 of IAS had no corresponding or equivalent Kenyan standard.

Prior to adopting international accounting and auditing standards, ICPAK, through its professional standards committee, undertook extensive consultations with ICPAK members, preparers, the banks and various regulators, in particular those in charge of the stock exchange. The committee issued various technical guidelines aimed at educating members on the differences between the Kenyan standards that were in use at the time and the international standards. Various technical seminars were also held to prepare for the full-scale adoption of international standards. In addition, a technical desk was set up to help deal with any queries arising when preparing financial statements. ICPAK also made arrangements to offer the books on the standards to members at reasonable rates. Various videos on accounting and auditing standards were obtained and shared with members through joint video sessions, after which these videos were made available in a technical library. Members were free to borrow and make use of these videos and other resource materials that were assembled to aid the adoption process.

Since the adoption of international standards, there have been various benefits. There has been enhanced comparability of financial statements and the provision of better financial information that facilitates analysis and decision-making by various users. The stock market has witnessed increased activity and there have also been more cross-border investments. The use of international reporting and auditing standards provides safeguards to the public and generally increases public confidence in financial reporting. There has been increased reliance by the regulators on financial reports which provide them a fairly reliable oversight mechanism.

Status of compliance with international financial reporting standards among Kenyan companies

In a bid to establish and encourage the use of IFRS, ICPAK established the Financial Reporting Award in 2002. This award involves the evaluation of financial statements which have been voluntarily submitted by companies, to gauge their compliance with the requirements of IFRS. In 2005, six years after implementation of the IFRS in Kenya, there was no single company which exhibited 100 per cent compliance with IFRS out of a total of 84 companies who submitted their financial statements for review. The 2005 compliance levels are shown in the table below, where 100 per cent denotes full compliance with all the requirements of IFRS including disclosure requirements.

Compliance with international reporting standards recognized by the 2005 Financial Reporting Award[54]

Compliance levels achieved (%)	Number of companies achieving the compliance levels				
	Insurance sector	Banking sector	All other companies	Total	
				No.	%
Above 80	3	0	10	13	16
60–79	12	10	15	37	44
50–59	7	1	3	11	13
Below 50	3	15	5	23	27
Total No.	25	26	33	84	100

As can be seen from the above table, while Kenya adopted the use of IFRS in 1999, levels of non-compliance are quite high. This is especially the case when you consider that the above companies were relatively large and, indeed, about 45 of them are listed on the Nairobi Stock Exchange. These companies have the resources to recruit well-trained professionals and, in the case of the listed ones, are required to comply with IFRS when preparing financial statements. In the light of the above, it can be expected that the level of compliance among the other private companies and small and medium-sized enterprises is likely to be quite low.

The Financial Reporting Award helps ICPAK to understand the areas of weaknesses in financial reporting and to design mechanisms to address these weaknesses. In early 2006, for example, various training sessions were organized focusing on presentation of financial statements and disclosure requirements of IAS 1 and 8. This training attracted about 300 participants and was well-received. However, it should be noted that ICPAK has adopted the approach of encouraging compliance rather than instigating disciplinary measures against those companies not in compliance.

Areas of non-compliance with international financial reporting standards among Kenyan companies

According to the evaluation of the annual reports submitted for the 2005 Financial Reporting Award, the following were the key areas of non-compliance with the best practices promulgated in the IFRS when preparing the financial reports:

IAS 1 – Presentation of financial Statements

Offsetting: IAS 1 provides that assets and liabilities, and income and expenses should not be offset unless required or permitted by a particular standard or an interpretation. Offsetting may

---

[54] **Based on data compiled by ICPAK.**

inhibit users' understanding of the substance of transactions and events that have occurred and prevent them from accurately assessing the entity's future cash-flows. Contrary to the above requirements, it was observed that some companies were netting off various items in the income statement, even where this was not permitted by any standard.

Identification of the financial statements: IAS 1 provides that financial statements and each component of financial statements should be identified clearly and distinguished from other information in the same published annual report or document. IFRS apply only to financial statements and it is therefore important that users are able to distinguish information prepared using IFRS from all other information presented in the annual reports that, while useful to users, is not subject to the requirements of IFRS. Annual reports should therefore clearly identify and distinguish what constitutes the financial statements either in the table of contents or elsewhere in the report. IAS 1 (p. 46) further provides that the name of the reporting entity or any other means of identification should be displayed prominently. It was observed that, while companies generally included financial statements in the table of contents, it was not possible to distinguish these from other information in the annual report.

The following was information that should have been presented on the face of the balance sheet, income statement or in the notes and other disclosures but in some cases was not:

Provisions: IAS 1 provides that provisions made in the current period are one of the line items that must at least be included on the face of the balance sheet.

Reserves: IAS 1 provides that the nature and purpose of each reserve within equity should be disclosed either on the face of the balance sheet or in the notes to the accounts.

Gross revenue: IAS 1 requires that as a minimum the face of the income statement must include a line item presenting the revenue for the period. Non-compliance with this requirement was noted mainly in the insurance sector.

Dividends: IAS 1 requires disclosure either on the face of the income statement, or the statement of changes in equity or in the notes, of the amount of dividends recognized as distributions to shareholders during the period and the related amount per share. Furthermore, IAS 1 requires disclosures of the amounts of dividends that had been declared before the financial statements were authorized for issue but were not recognized as a distribution to shareholders during the period.

Domicile and country of incorporation: IAS 1 requires disclosure of the domicile, legal form of the enterprise and its country of incorporation.

IAS 2 – Inventories

Inventories: IAS requires disclosures of the accounting policies that have been adopted including the cost formulas used in determining the cost of inventories. In addition, the carrying amount of the inventories carried at net realizable value should be disclosed.

IAS 7 – Cash flow statements

Preparation of cash flow statements: IAS 7 requires preparation of a cash flow statement for the entity as a whole which shows how the company generates and uses cash and cash equivalents. It was observed that some companies presented cash flow information for only a section of the business rather than for the enterprise as a whole. For instance, an insurance company would present cash flows for only the general business and not the life business.

Acquisition of a subsidiary: IAS 7 requires that where a subsidiary was acquired during the period, the cash flow statement should clearly indicate the portion of the purchase price that was paid by means of cash and cash equivalents as well as the amount of cash and cash equivalents in the subsidiary that was acquired. It was observed that there were instances when an acquisition had occurred but this information was not disclosed.

IAS 12 – Income taxes

Deferred tax on revaluation: IAS 12 requires recognition of a deferred tax liability for all taxable temporary differences. IAS 12 further notes that sometimes an asset is revalued and this revaluation does not affect the taxable profit for the current period. In such a case, the future recovery of the asset's carrying amount will result in a taxable flow of economic benefits to the entity and the amount deductible for tax purposes will differ from the amount of those economic benefits. The difference between the carrying amount of the revalued asset and its tax base is a temporary difference and therefore gives rise to a deferred tax liability that should be recognized. In most cases, this was not being done.

IAS 14 – Segment reporting

Segment reporting: IAS 14 establishes the principles for reporting financial information by segment and should be applied by all those entities whose equity or debt securities are publicly traded. Those entities whose securities are not publicly traded but who choose to disclose segmental information voluntarily in financial statements that comply with IFRS, should comply fully with the requirements of IAS 14. Many companies, both listed and non-listed, which presented segmental information failed to comply fully with the requirements of IAS 14.

IAS 16: Property, plant and equipment

Revaluation of property, plant and equipment: IAS 16 requires that an increase in the asset's carrying amount resulting from revaluations should be credited directly to equity under the heading "revaluation surplus". This was sometimes not being done and instead the revaluation surplus would be credited to reserves.

Disclosures: IAS 16 requires that where items of property, plant and equipment are stated at revalued amounts, the following information should be disclosed: the frequency of revaluations, restriction on distribution of revaluation surpluses and the carrying amount of the revalued class of property, plant and equipment, had the assets been carried under the cost model. In most cases, it was observed that this was not being done by companies. The disclosures were mainly regarding the effective date of revaluation and the involvement of independent and professional valuers.

IAS 17 – Leases

Operating leases: IAS 17 requires the following disclosures with respect to operating leases: the total of future minimum lease payments under non-cancellable operating leases for each of the following periods (not later than one year, later than one year and not later than five years, and later than five years). This was not being done.

IAS 19 – Employment benefits

Retirement benefit obligations: IAS 19 sets out various disclosures that should be made with respect to defined benefit plans, which were not made by most companies.

IAS 24 – Related party disclosures

Related party transactions: IAS 24 provides that, if there have been transactions between related parties, then disclosures must be made on the nature of the related party relationships, the types and elements of transactions entered into so as to ensure better understanding of financial statements. In some cases, the disclosures that were made were not as complete or comprehensive as they should be.

IAS 30 – Disclosures in the financial statements of banks and similar financial institutions

Concentration of deposit liabilities: IAS 30 requires banks to disclose any significant concentrations of their assets, liabilities and off-balance-sheet items. Such disclosures should be made in terms of geographical areas, customer or industry groups or other concentrations of risk. In addition, the amount of significant net foreign currency exposures should also be disclosed. These disclosures are a useful indication of the potential risks inherent in the realization of the assets and the funds available to the bank. Many banks have not yet complied with this requirement.

Assets pledged as security: IAS 30 requires banks to disclose the aggregate amount of secured liabilities and the nature and carrying amount of the assets pledged as security. This is because at times banks are required to pledge assets as security to support certain deposits and other liabilities. The amounts involved are often substantial and may have a significant impact on the assessment of the financial position of a bank. Many banks have not yet complied with this requirement.

IAS 33 – Earnings per share

Measurement: IAS 33 requires computation of basic and diluted earnings per share by dividing the profit or adjusted profit attributable to ordinary shareholders as the numerator by the weighted average number of ordinary shares outstanding or as adjusted during the period as the denominator. The computed basic and diluted earnings per share should be presented on the face of the income statement for each class of ordinary shares that has a different right to share in the net profit for the period in accordance with IAS 33. The amounts used as numerators and a reconciliation of those amounts to the net profit or loss for the period as well as denominators should be disclosed in accordance with IAS 33.

IAS 32 – Financial instruments (disclosures and presentation) and IAS 39 – Financial instruments (recognition and measurement)

Disclosures: IAS 32 requires various disclosures to be made so as to enhance understanding of the significance of financial instruments to an entity's financial position, performance and cash flows and assist in assessing the amounts, timing and certainty of future cash flows associated with those instruments. To that effect, companies should describe their financial-risk-management objectives and policies and provide information that will enable users assess the extent of market, credit, liquidity and cash-flow interest-rate risk related to financial instruments. This concept is further reiterated in IAS 39. Various disclosures as required by both IAS 32 and IAS 39 were not done. For example, it was observed that companies did not give information on how fair value was determined or the fair values of those financial assets and liabilities carried at amortized cost. Banks also did not disclose the interest income accrued on impaired loans and not yet received in cash.

In conclusion, it was noted that most companies lacked clear policies on the recognition criteria, the classification for measurement purposes and the treatment of gains or losses on disposal of various financial instruments. Where there were policies these tended to be quite general and were therefore not useful in enhancing understating of the financial statements.

Accounting policies

IAS 1 requires disclosure of both the measurement basis used in preparing financial statements and all other significant accounting policies used by the company that would be relevant to understanding the financial statements. In particular, companies should disclose those policies that are selected from alternatives allowed in standards and interpretation. In addition, those policies that have the most significant effect on the amounts recognized in the financial statements and any judgments used in applying such policies should be disclosed. As a general rule, disclosure of accounting policies used should be made where such disclosure would assist users in understanding how transactions, other events and conditions are reflected in the reported financial performance and financial position.

It was observed that there were areas where companies failed to disclose the accounting policies used even when the circumstances were such that disclosure was warranted. These areas included: policies on consolidation principles; borrowings; components of cash and cash equivalents; leases; and de-recognition of financial instruments and employee benefits where it was noted that most companies with defined benefit plans made no disclosures on the accounting policy for recognizing actuarial gains and losses.

Voluntary disclosures

Disclosures are usually of two types: mandatory and voluntary. Mandatory disclosures are those required by financial reporting standards. Voluntary disclosures are those that represent additional information over and above what is required by reporting standards. Such disclosures provide greater understanding of the financial position and liquidity of the enterprise.

As part of the 2005 Financial Reporting Award, recognition was given to those companies which had made significant disclosures voluntarily. Some of the areas where voluntary disclosures were made included segment reporting by those companies that are not listed and for whom segmental reporting is therefore not mandatory. Other voluntary disclosures noted related to property, plant and equipment, where some companies disclosed the gross carrying amount of fully depreciated property, plant and equipment still in use and the carrying amount of temporarily idle property, plant and equipment. Some companies also made disclosures on those fully amortized intangible assets that were still in use. Such disclosures were positive, as they did enhance the value of the financial statements to users.

Reasons for the non-compliance with international financial reporting standards among Kenyan companies

One of the reasons for non-compliance includes the growing complexity of IFRS. IFRS have become increasingly more complex and subjective in recent years, requiring technical expertise for their understanding and implementation. There have been frequent and rapid changes to various standards arising from improvements and convergence projects. The improvement project gave rise to simultaneous amendments to 13 standards, while the convergence project led to various changes to standards, for example, those on presentation of financial statements, accounting policies and changes in accounting estimates and errors.

The move towards the fair value model has also introduced complications. It is a subjective concept and is difficult to implement, particularly in developing economies like Kenya. This has particularly been problematic for those in the financial services sector and, as can be seen from the above table, the sector that seems to exhibit the highest levels of non-compliance is the banking sector. Fair value has been defined as the amount for which an asset could be exchanged, or a liability settled, between knowledgeable, willing parties in an arm's length transaction. However, while the concept is easy to understand, determination of fair value has been very difficult and at times impossible.

In Kenya, fair valuation of financial instrument, including bonds and derivatives, has been very difficult because of a lack of reliable market information. The Kenyan capital market is still in its infancy and cannot be relied on to determine fair value for the financial instruments. Auditors in Kenya lack reliable accurate points of reference for some instruments.

There are also cases of conflict between the requirements of IFRS, particularly with regard to fair valuations, and those of various regulations and legislation. In Kenya, there have been instances where the regulator has refused to accept fair valuations based on IAS. An example of this is the determination of provisioning using the methodology prescribed by the Central Bank for use by the banking sector and provisioning as per IFRS. The Central Bank of Kenya has issued a guideline CBK/ on risk classification of assets and provisioning, known as guideline No. 10. Section 5 (d) of this guideline on minimum provisioning allocations is very specific as to the minimum percentage amounts that banks should use to compute provisions. As far as ICPAK can determine, these rates recommended by the Central Bank of Kenya are arbitrary. ICPAK has recommended that the Central Bank allow banks to use IAS 39 to determine these provisions on the basis of each bank's roll rates and recovery experiences for portfolio loans. In addition, for significant individual loans, impairment should be determined on a case-by-case basis using discounted cash flows from repayments and the security provided.

In general, there is need for further discussions on the use of fair values. Absence of accurate, reliable data on discount rates volatility, industry or company data to support cash-flow trends, crop yields, loan yields, loan default rates and lack of markets or underdevelopment of the existing ones has made the situation worse. There is need to establish which items can be measured at fair values and which items cannot. Establishing sector benchmarks will also help in determining of fair values for some items.

The issuance of IFRS 4 on insurance contracts introduced further complication into financial reporting for the sector. Previously, the insurance sector prepared separate income statements for long-term and short-term businesses. This practice was now challenged resulting in opposition from many stakeholders in the industry. The need to provide comparative information, especially for some items, also posed difficulties for the preparers.

There were conflicts between the reporting requirements of IFRS 4 and those of the Insurance Act. For instance, the Act is explicit on the methods to be applied by insurance companies when calculating claims reserves in respect of general insurance business. Thus, when computing the amounts of provisions for claims incurred but not reported, the Insurance Act prescribes certain minimum percentages to be used depending on the levels of net written premiums. These percentages are to be used by all insurance companies. In contrast, IFRS 4 requires that the percentages to be used should be determined from the respective insurance company's past experience which may indicate lower rates.

There was further conflict with the insurance sector regulator in Kenya with regard to the IFRS 4 approach to determining taxable profit for life business, especially due to the difficulties posed by unbundling of contracts between the (deposit) investment component and the insurance component. Reporting surpluses in the profit and loss account that are not available for distribution to shareholders has been a major concern in the industry.

To tackle the challenges being faced in the insurance sector, ICPAK prepared specimen financial statements demonstrating the application of IFRS 4 to the sector. In preparing these statements, ICAK involved the various stakeholders, including the insurance regulator and the Association of Kenya Insurers, an umbrella association that represents the various insurance companies. Nevertheless, because various reports to the insurance regulator are prescribed in the Insurance Act, the regulator did indicate that, while insurance companies would generally be expected to produce IFRS-compliant financial statements, they would also prepare returns to the regulator in accordance with the Act and where the differences between the returns and the financial statements, appropriate reconciliations would be prepared and reviewed by the auditors.

Nevertheless, it should be noted that the insurance regulator does not have the resources and capacity to review the financial statements submitted by the various insurance companies and determine the level of compliance with IFRS.

There were also difficulties in enforcing compliance with the requirements of IAS 17 on leases. The requirement to separate land from buildings was difficult to implement, particularly where the cost of land and the buildings were not carried separately in the books of the entity. It was difficult to determine which cost to apportion to land and which to buildings, especially where these had been bought for a single consideration and were carried at cost. The recommended method of apportioning costs between land and buildings would entail additional costs, such as use of professional valuers.

IAS 17 on leases was also challenged by the regulators and the preparers for a number of reasons. In some cases, companies which had classified leasehold land as long term were required to reclassify them as operating leases, given the lease terms. In such circumstances, these companies were required to write back revaluation gains. Furthermore, once the leases had been reclassified, the prepaid operating lease rentals would have to be amortized over the life of the lease, whereas previously these leases were considered long term and not depreciated. The immediate impact of this was to reduce reported profits, although this was minimal where the leases were for a period of say 999 years. The greater impact though was the implications on capital adequacy, particularly for banks and insurance companies which had strict levels of capital adequacy set by the various regulators. Indeed, the impact on core capital for the banking institutions holding land on leases that were nearing termination was significant, since prior-period adjustments to reserves were for the entire cost of these leases. To reduce the impact of this, some banking institutions had to dispose of non-core assets such as leasehold land and buildings, particularly those that were being held as investments.

The treatment of unrealized reserves has also been of concern to regulators. For example, IAS 40 on investment property does allow the gain or loss from the change in the fair value of investment property to be recognized in the profit and loss for the period in which it arises. This has prompted concerns by regulators that this may create a loophole by means of which companies may manipulate their performances. The insurance regulator was quick to issue a circular to all insurance companies which explained how the unrealized reserves should be treated. This circular indicated that only 50 per cent of unrealized reserves could be distributed as dividends and the remainder was to be capitalized.

At the same time, there were concerns among preparers that reflecting unrealized gains through profit and loss may lead to taxation by the tax authorities. This is an area that has yet to be resolved and ICPAK has engaged the tax authorities on the taxation of such unrealized gains with a view to eventually developing an appropriate guideline on the matter.

Status of implementation of auditing standards

In 2004, ICPAK embarked on a quality review programme, the intention being to review audit firms to determine audit firms' compliance with auditing standards. A pilot review of seven firms was carried out by a team from IPAK in 2004 and early 2005. Another 18 audit firms were reviewed in 2005.

The results of the pilot reviews were not encouraging. There were significant deficiencies in the application of auditing standards by the audit firms; in particular, it was found that there was no documentation of the audit process and audit files maintained were incomplete. There was also non-compliance with IFRS, notably: IAS 1 on presentation of financial statements, IAS 12 on income taxes, IAS 17 on leases, IAS 16 on property plant and equipment, IAS 39 on recognition and measurement of financial instruments and IAS 40 on investment property. The reasons for non-compliance in these areas have been discussed earlier.

Other weaknesses noted included a general lack of evidence to demonstrate understanding and application of quality control and little documentation of quality control policies and procedures. Nor was there much evidence of compliance with professional auditing standards, in particular: ISAs 250, 260, 300, 315, 400, 505, 520 and 610 encompassing the entire planning process; ISA 220 (particularly as regards the review of the firm's independence); ISA 530 on sampling; ISA 545 as regards fair value; ISA 570 as regards going concerns; and ISA 560 regarding post-balance-sheet events. It was also found that there was poor documentation of entire audit process, in particular in gathering and recording procedures and the audit evidence sought, conclusions arrived at and the reporting results. Generally, there was poor documentation on the basis of overall audit opinion and a failure to issue the various standard letters used in audit, including engagement letters, letters of representation, official clearance from outgoing auditor and the comprehensive audit plan.

The feedback received from the firms reviewed was that there was need for comprehensive training to help audit practitioners to appreciate and understand the auditing process. A decision was therefore taken to develop a training module for audit practitioners and this was done in 2005. The programme targeting audit partners and owners of audit firms was highly subsidized by ICPAK. ICPAK charged each participant an equivalent of $150 for the three-day non-residential training. By the end of 2005, about 350 practitioners had taken the training programme and there was improvement in the results of the audit quality reviews.

Nonetheless, the practitioners asked ICPAK to develop a similar programme for their audit staff and assist in producing audit manuals and even a sample audit file that the firms could use in their audit work. ICPAK embarked on these projects and it is expected that the training will commence in the latter half of 2006, when the manuals and reference materials should be completed.

In 2006, ICPAK also launched the fully fledged audit reviews, with a target of 130 audit firms slated for review that year. While there have been slight improvements, it is envisaged that the results of the training will only be evident in 2007 and subsequent years. Only then can the level of compliance with auditing standards be gauged.

IV. Lessons learned in the implementation process

The key to increasing the compliance levels is to guarantee trained persons who understand the use of IFRS and ISA. This requires that the qualification process emphasizes proficiency in the use of the various standards. In Kenya, given that the body in charge of the qualification process is different from ICPAK, which is essentially the standard-setting body, there may be difficulties in ensuring the qualification process keeps up with the developments in the standards. Traditionally, it takes a very long time to change or review syllabuses to keep up with the changes to the standards over the past few years. The training of accountants is also two-fold; there are academic programmes offered by universities and professional programmes. In Kenya, there is no mechanism to coordinate the two different types of training and ensure that both keep up with changes in the accountancy profession. There is no linkage between the universities, KASNEB and ICPAK and this is an area that needs to be addressed. Having said that, it should also be noted that the number of qualified accountants is quite low in Kenya; only about 10,000 fully qualified accountants as at 31 December 2005.

In addition, a majority of preparers of financial statements do not have access to the standards and do not keep up-to-date with the standards and various developments. While ICPAK tries to provide the standards, the cost is prohibitive for most preparers and auditors. ICPAK requires its members to acquire a certain number of hours of training per year. However, statistics indicate that majority of ICPAK members do not adhere to these requirements. The reason for non-adherence to the continuing professional education requirements is usually related to the cost of the various seminars and workshops organized by ICPAK. This is a particular problem for those whose employers do not meet the cost of the seminars and workshops. In addition, in prior years, ICPAK did not have the necessary mechanism to enforce learning requirements. There was no consequence of not meeting the minimum learning requirements. However, with effect from 2006, the ICPAK council decided that one of the criteria to be used in evaluating a member's standing with ICPAK would be attainment of the minimum learning requirements prescribed by the council. Thus, any member who requests a letter of good standing from ICPAK and who has not completed the minimum training hours for 2005 is required to make a written commitment to making up for the deficiency in 2006. ICAPK has also embarked on a campaign to foster a commitment to lifelong learning amongst its members. This campaign includes making presentations during various ICPAK events and publishing articles in the ICPAK bimonthly journal which emphasize the importance of developing a culture of lifelong learning.

ICPAK has also provided increased training and user support to ensure that its members fully understand the standards and can implement them without difficulty. However, ICPAK has faced challenges in accessing competent resource persons and, at the same time, ensuring that the training sessions are affordable to all. In 2005, for example, ICPAK launched a series of training sessions on audit quality assurance. These were aimed at providing basic understanding of auditing techniques to practitioners and were highly subsidized by ICPAK.

ICPAK itself needs to increase the technical support offered to members and has therefore committed itself to building its technical capacity. However, this process is constrained by a lack of resources. ICPAK strives to develop various guides and sample financial statements to aid in the understanding of standards. This process is sometimes slow given the scarcity of resource persons who understand the issues enough to ensure production of guides that are simple yet comprehensive. This is an area where standard-setters can harness their collective resources and share the work on the guides among themselves – even perhaps at a regional level.

In Kenya, the vast majority of companies can be considered to be SMEs. They are largely owner-managed or controlled with financial statements produced largely for use by banks and tax authorities. In most cases, they lack a well-developed finance function and do not employ qualified accountants due to a lack of resources. Since they are managed by their owners, SMEs are not motivated to adhere to the reporting requirements of IFRS. Indeed, the more complex the standards, the less likely that SMEs will understand them and the higher the levels of non-compliance. The IASB project on reporting for SMEs should be expedited, while still giving due consideration to the fact that SMEs are defined differently in developed countries than they are in developing countries. A highly simplified set of standards is perhaps necessary for SMEs in developing countries.

To anticipate changes in standards, there is need for increased participation in standard-setting. This may not be possible at the level of each individual institute but can be done through regional bodies, such as the Eastern Central and Southern African Federation of Accountants in the case of African countries. Increased participation would ensure that implementation challenges are anticipated prior to finalization of standards. In fact, regulators should be involved where the proposed standards will impact on the industries they regulate at all stages of the standard-setting process. This will, however, not be easy given that the regulators themselves are constrained and do not have personnel with the expertise to understand and appreciate reporting standards.

V. Conclusion

A financial reporting system supported by high-quality standards, such as IFRS and ISAs, is central to economic development. Increased levels of globalization are underscoring the important role of a common financial reporting framework supported by strong globally accepted financial reporting standards. However, the implementation of the standards will continue to be problematic. This can be attested by the fact that, even after seven years since the adoption of IFRS and ISAs in Kenya, compliance levels remain relatively low among companies in Kenya.

A multi-pronged approach is required to enhance adoption of international reporting and auditing standards. The focus should be on simplifying the standards themselves and creating a stable platform or period during which no new standards are issued until the existing ones have been well and thoroughly understood. The different reporting needs of various categories of companies, including those of SMEs must be recognized. These require a highly simplified set of standards to encourage compliance at these levels. For the developing economies, a majority of the population's interactions with the economy occurs at the micro and small-size firm level and, if there can be an appreciation of the importance of good financial reporting at these levels, albeit based on simplified but nevertheless high quality standards, then the impact of sound financial reporting will no doubt cascade to the rest of the economy.

The education process needs to be addressed, as this equips preparers and auditors with the tools they need to understand and participate in the financial reporting process using IFRS and ISAs. In this case, the education process should comprise both the pre- and post-accountancy qualification phases. Accountants need to continuously review and enhance their skills set so as to remain relevant. In this regard, professional bodies must be strengthened so as to ensure that their members remain relevant and committed to the adoption and compliance with international reporting standards.

Ultimately, those pursuing the implementation of IFRS need to be relentless, however daunting the challenge may seem.

Chapter VII

Case study of Pakistan

I. Introduction[1]

A. Overview of economic indicators

With a population of about 160 million, Pakistan's economy delivered yet another year (2006/07) of solid economic growth – of 7 per cent – despite the continuing surge in oil prices that created adverse effects on its trade balance. Achieving gross domestic product (GDP) growth of around 7 per cent over the last five years indicates that Pakistan's upbeat momentum remains on track as it maintains its position as one of the fastest growing economies in Asian region, along with China, India and Viet Nam.

Foreign direct investment in Pakistan is expected to reach $6 billion[2] in fiscal year 2007 compared to around $3 billion the previous year. International investors call for comparable financial information from countries competing for foreign investments. This requires that the corporate sector in Pakistan comply with internationally acceptable standards on financial reporting. Pakistan, which currently has about 660 listed companies, has created a statutory framework to regulate business activities, including regulatory institutions for enforcing accounting and auditing standards. In order to ensure high-quality corporate financial reporting, appropriate enforcement mechanisms have been put in place.

B. Requirements relating to implementation of international financial reporting standards

With regard to compliance with IFRS, the Securities and Exchange Commission of Pakistan (SECP) is empowered under section 234 of the Companies Ordinance to prescribe appropriate international accounting standards. SECP issues notifications of the accounting standards based on the recommendations of the Institute of Charted Accountants of Pakistan (ICAP).

IFRS considered appropriate to the local environment are adopted verbatim. Pakistan is among the few countries to have started following the International Accounting Standards (IAS) regime early. The ICAP council has been adopting IAS since the 1970s and, thanks to its efforts, notifications of 18 IAS were issued by SECP back in 1986.

C. Accounting framework in Pakistan

ICAP had issued the following revised statement to ensure compliance with the IAS/IFRS in its circular No. 01/2003 dated 24 February 2003:

---

[1] This document was prepared and edited by the UNCTAD secretariat on the basis of significant inputs provided by Mr. Syed Asad Ali Shah, Mr. Shahid Hussain and Ms. Maria Ahmed, from the Directorate of Technical Services of the Institute of Chartered Accountants of Pakistan.
[2] *Pakistan Economic and Strategic Outlook*. Global Investment House.

"These financial statements have been prepared in accordance with approved accounting standards as applicable in Pakistan and the requirements of Companies Ordinance, 1984. Approved accounting standards comprise of such International Accounting Standards as notified under the provisions of the Companies Ordinance, 1984. Wherever the requirements of the Companies Ordinance, 1984 or directives issued by the Securities and Exchange Commission of Pakistan differ with the requirements of these standards, the requirements of Companies Ordinance, 1984 or the requirements of the said directives take precedence."

In some situations, accounting technical releases are formulated where IFRS do not deal with a certain issue specific to the local environment or where additional guidance is required. These are mainly formulated in line with the principles laid out in IFRS. Departures from the requirements of IFRS are avoided as far as possible. The Companies Ordinance of 1984 also prescribes presentation and disclosure requirements. Additionally, the State Bank of Pakistan, which regulates the commercial banks and development finance institutions, prescribes the recognition and measurement requirement in respect of loans, advances and investments.

D. Due process for adoption of IFRS

ICAP, a statutory body established under the Chartered Accountants Ordinance of 1962 is the regulator of the accountancy profession in Pakistan. All public companies are required to have their financial statements audited by chartered accountants who are members of ICAP. All members of ICAP are required to comply with the professional standards covering accounting, auditing and ethical pronouncements. ICAP has been adopting IFRS issued by the International Accounting Standards Board and international standards on auditing (ISAs) issued by the International Auditing and Assurance Standards Board for over 20 years. ICAP has also adopted the Code of Ethics issued by the ethics board of the International Federation of Accountants.

ICAP has established a due process of technical review and consultation by setting up various committees which review IFRS, disseminate the exposure drafts to the corporate sector and its members, and consult with the stakeholders and then recommend to its council adoption of a particular standard.

After completion of the due process, the ICAP council recommends that SECP adopt a particular standard. Thereafter, after undergoing its internal deliberations and review process, SECP issues notification of the adoption of such standards for listed companies.

It may be noted that, through the above process, Pakistan has been adopting IFRS without making any amendments in such standards.

E. Council's strategy for IFRS

While in the past, the ICAP council and SECP have adopted most IAS, so as to make Pakistan generally accepted accounting principles (GAAP) largely based on such international standards, the ICAP council has decided that ICAP will work together with SECP and the State Bank of Pakistan to ensure that Pakistan GAAP become fully compliant with IFRS, as far as public interest entities are concerned, by the end of 2009. For this purpose, the Professional Standards and Technical Advisory Committee has formed a committee to carry out a detailed gap analysis, especially in terms of identifying inconsistencies between the prevailing law and the requirements of IFRS.

F. Current status of adoption of IFRS

Pakistan has made significant progress in closing the gap between local requirements for corporate financial reporting and international standards, by not only adopting IFRS, but also establishing mechanisms to ensure their enforcement. Over the past few years, this has contributed to significant improvement in corporate financial reporting.

At the time of the Reports on Observance of Standards and Codes review that was carried out by the Word Bank in 2005, all IAS had been adopted by ICAP and the relevant notification for listed companies issued by SECP except IAS 29 on financial reporting in hyperinflationary economies and IAS 41 on agriculture, and IFRS 1–6. Since then, on the recommendation of ICAP, SECP has issued notification of IAS 41, IFRS 2, IFRS 3, IFRS 5 and IFRS 6.

In the case of the banking sector, on the recommendation of the Pakistan Banks' Association and ICAP, the State Bank of Pakistan has suspended the application of IAS 39 and IAS 40. However, SBP has agreed in principle with ICAP that these standards, together with other IFRS, will also be adopted over the next two years, so as to ensure that banks and financial institutions' financial reporting becomes fully compliant with IFRS.

G. Three-tiered structure and standards for small and medium-sized enterprises

The mandatory application of all IFRS for all companies tends to burden small and medium-sized enterprises (SMEs). Given the substantial volume and complexities of IFRS, it is not possible for SMEs to ensure full compliance with all the requirements of IFRS. In reality, these SMEs do not have adequate technical capabilities and resources to ensure compliance with complicated reporting requirements.

While ICAP has been pursuing the objective of adoption and use of international standards for the preparation of general-purpose financial statements over the years, it also recognizes the difficulties faced by SMEs in complying with the full set of IFRS that have been made applicable for listed companies.

To address the needs of SMEs, the ICAP council initiated a project to develop a separate set of standards for such entities in line with similar work done in various other countries as well as the Accounting and Financial Reporting Guidelines for Small and Medium-sized Enterprises issued by UNCTAD through ISAR in 2003. After several months of research on SME accounting standards by its committees, ICAP has developed two SME standards: an accounting and financial reporting standard for medium-sized entities and an accounting and financial reporting standard for small-sized entities. The council has also laid down a three-tiered framework of accounting standards, as described below.

The ICAP council approved the aforementioned three-tiered structure and the two SME standards at its meeting on 28 July 2006, and it is expected that SECP will shortly issue notification these standards and three-tiered structure as part of the law, as the framework and the standards were developed in consultation with SECP, which has in principle agreed to incorporate these requirements as part of the statute applicable to all companies.

Pakistan's initiative for developing standards for SMEs was recognized by the South Asian Federation of Accountants (comprising professional accounting bodies of Bangladesh, India, Nepal, Pakistan and Sri Lanka), which has adopted these standards as standards/guidelines.

ICAP has suggested the three-tiered structure as shown in table 1 for the applicability of these standards.

Table 1. Three-tiered structure for SME standards

Tier 1	Publicly interest entities (listed entities, entities that are considered large and entities that have public accountability)	The complete set of IFRS that is approved by the ICAP council and for which notification has been issued by SECP shall be applicable to these entities.
Tier 2	Medium-sized entities (entities that are neither public interest entities nor small-sized entities)	The accounting and financial reporting framework and standard for medium-sized entities issued by ICAP are applicable to these entities.
Tier 3	Small-sized entities (small entities that have turnover and paid-up capital below specified threshold)	The accounting and financial reporting framework and standard for small-sized entities issued by ICAP are applicable to these entities.

H. Impediments in implementing IFRS

While the ICAP council is committed to complying with the full set of IFRS by 2009 so as to enable all public interest entities to give unreserved compliance with all IFRS issued by the International Accounting Standards Board, there are various impediments and difficulties in achieving such compliance which are being addressed, some of which are indicated below.

Historically, there have remained some provisions in the Companies Ordinance and other local laws that are inconsistent with the requirements of IFRS. ICAP has been working with the regulators to remove such inconsistencies, and has had reasonable success in recent years. Nevertheless, it takes significant time to reach agreement with regulators and also get the amendments incorporated through the legislative process.

Some of the IFRS – such as IAS 39, IAS 19, IFRS 3, etc. – are quite complex. Because of limited capacity available in Pakistan in terms of understanding, interpreting and training on the subject of such IFRS, preparers require more time in implementing such standards.

Because of limited capacity available with the regulators, and frequent changes at key positions, it takes considerable time to persuade the regulators to adopt IFRS.

Although the State Bank of Pakistan has agreed to full implementation of IAS 39 and IAS 40, some of the preparers (some banks and financial institutions) are still not fully convinced of their adoption. Resistance from such stakeholders may further delay full implementation of IFRS.

There is a shortage of facilities for training and continuing education on IFRS.

I. Compliance gaps between international financial reporting standards and local statutes

At present, there are certain requirements of Companies Ordinance, its fourth schedule (this contains disclosure requirements for listed companies) and SECP directives that are in conflict with the requirements of IFRS.

The developments in this regard included revision of the fourth schedule to the Companies Ordinance issued by SECP on 5 July 2004, after which almost all the conflicting requirements and duplications have been eliminated.

Compliance gaps that still exist between IFRS and local statutes are summarized in table 2.

Table 2. Gaps between IFRS and local statutes

Companies Ordinance	IAS/IFRS
Surplus on revaluation of fixed assets shown in the balance sheet after capital and reserves.	Credited directly to equity under the heading of revaluation surplus (IAS 16.37).
Redeemable preference share classified as "Subscribed share capital". Redemption allowed only out of profits.	Classified as financial liability if it provides for mandatory redemption by the issuer for a fixed or determinable amount at a fixed or determinable future date, etc. (IAS 32.22).

SECP Directive	IAS/IFRS
To facilitate application of the revised fourth schedule, transitional relaxation has been granted by SECP to listed companies for the following items:	
The listed companies carrying deferred cost as on 5 July 2004 are allowed to treat such cost as per superseded fourth schedule. However, after that date, any further deferral of costs will not be allowed.	The concept of deferred cost no longer exists in IAS/IFRS.
The listed companies having outstanding liabilities for foreign currency loans as on 5 July 2004 are allowed to capitalize fluctuation of exchange gain/loss as per superseded fourth schedule up to 30 September 2007. Any exchange gain/loss on foreign currency loan contracted on or after 5 July 2004 will not be allowed to be capitalized.	The revised IAS 21 (the effects of changes in foreign exchange rates, effective 1 January 2005) has withdrawn the requirement of the old IAS 21, which allowed capitalization of exchange differences resulting from a severe devaluation or depreciation of currency.

In addition to the above, prudential regulations issued by the State Bank of Pakistan also include certain requirements that are in conflict with IAS 39. Some examples of impediments to adoption of IAS 39 are given below:

- Banks and development financial institutions are required to use age criteria (the number of days default/overdue mark-up/interest or principal) for the purpose of determining loan loss provisions, rather than estimating the expected cash flows in terms of IAS 39.

- Unquoted securities are stated at cost.

- Staff loans are recorded at the amount of cash disbursed and income on such loans is recorded at the subsidized rates.

- Since many of the financial assets are required to be valued on a mark-to-market basis with changes in fair value being recognized in profit and loss, it results in recognition of unrealized gains and losses. Since recognition of unrealized gains could become taxable, banks and financial institutions are reluctant to adopt this standard. This is considered a major impediment to implementation of this standard.

ICAP, as part of its strategy, has been persuading both SECP and the State Bank of Pakistan to eliminate barriers to the adoption of IAS/IFRS.

As discussed above, ICAP has developed and issued two separate sets of accounting and financial reporting standards for SMEs. The notification of the standards must be issued by SECP before they will apply to SMEs.

In December 2006, SECP on the recommendation of ICAP, issued notification of the following IAS/IFRS:

- IAS 41 – Agriculture;
- IFRS 2 – Share-based payments;
- IFRS 3 – Business combinations;
- IFRS 5 – Non-current assets held for sale and discontinued operations; and
- IFRS 6 – Exploration for and evaluation of mineral resources.

To ensure effective implementation of SME standards, a revision of the fifth schedule to the Companies Ordinance (which prescribes presentation and disclosure requirements for non-listed public entities and private entities) is under way. Efforts are being made to remove all requirements from the schedule that are in conflict with the SME standards.

Regarding adoption of remaining IFRS/IAS (i.e. IFRS 1, 4, 7 and 8; and IAS 29 and IAS 40), the following strategies and action plans have been decided by ICAP:

(1) IFRS 1 will be adopted once all other IAS/IFRS are adopted.

(2) Previously, adoption of IFRS 4 was deferred until finalization of phase II of the International Accounting Standards Board's insurance project, as it would necessitate some amendments to the Insurance Ordinance of 2000 and Regulations. However, it has recently been decided that, instead of waiting for the completion of phase II of the project, ICAP will consider the standard for adoption. The insurance committee of ICAP is actively deliberating on the adoption of this standard.

(3) ICAP has approved the adoption of IFRS 7 and ICAP has recommended that SECP issue notification.

(4) IFRS 8 is applicable for the accounting periods beginning on or after January 2009 and its adoption by ICAP is expected shortly after the standard supersedes IAS 14 on segment reporting, which had already adopted in Pakistan.

(5) IAS 29 was not previously adopted because it was not considered relevant in the country's economic environment. However, the matter of adoption of IAS 29 is under consideration by ICAP on the premise that there might be instances where a Pakistani company operates in or transacts with an entity of a hyperinflationary economy, in which case the standard could become applicable.

(6) In the Finance Act 2007–2008, the taxation laws have been amended so that the adjustments that are made to the financial statements of the bank to comply with the requirements of IAS 39 on financial instruments (recognition and measurement) and IAS 40 on investment property have been allowed to be excluded while calculating the taxable income of banks. These exclusions have been allowed to safeguard the bank from being taxed on unrealized gains, as the above standards require measurement and recognition of financial instrument and investment property on the basis of their fair market value prevailing on the balance sheet date.

(7) IAS 40 allows investment property to be measured either at cost or fair value. Therefore, if a bank or development financial institution chose the fair value model, it could distribute unrealized gains arising out of an upward revaluation of investment property, which is not considered appropriate by the regulator (the State Bank). This matter has been addressed through an appropriate amendment introduced through Finance Act 2007 to the existing section 248 (2) of the Companies Ordinance by restricting all the corporate entities to paying dividends out of their realized profits only (as is the case under United Kingdom company law). It is expected that after this amendment, the deferment of IAS 40 by the State Bank will be eliminated.

At the request of ICAP, SECP has also reissued notification of IAS (number and name only) for which notification was previously issued, by reproducing their full text. This step was taken to avoid lengthy process of adoption and notification each time an IAS is revised.

II. Regulatory framework and enforcement

A. Securities and Exchange Commission of Pakistan

The Securities and Exchange Commission of Pakistan (SECP) was set up in pursuance of the Securities and Exchange Commission of Pakistan Act of 1997 to succeed the Corporate Law Authority. This Act institutionalized certain policy decisions relating to the constitution, structure, powers and functions of SECP, thereby giving it administrative authority and financial independence in carrying out its regulatory and statutory responsibilities.

SECP became operational in January 1999. It was initially concerned with the regulation of the corporate sector and capital market. Over time, its mandate has expanded to include supervision and regulation of insurance companies, non-banking finance companies and private pensions. SECP has also been entrusted with oversight of various external service providers to the corporate and financial sectors, including chartered accountants, credit rating agencies, corporate secretaries, brokers, surveyors, etc. The challenge for SECP has grown with the increase of its mandate.

B. Companies Ordinance of 1984

The Companies Ordinance sets the primary requirements for financial reporting of all companies incorporated in Pakistan. The Companies Ordinance requires the preparation, presentation and publication of financial statements, including disclosures and auditing of all companies incorporated in Pakistan. In addition to the various provisions pertaining to financial reporting, the fourth schedule of the Ordinance lays down the form, content and certain disclosure requirements for preparing financial statements for listed companies, while the fifth schedule outlines the same for non-listed companies. As discussed above, various provisions of the Companies Ordinance, including the fourth schedule, have already been revised in compliance with the requirements of IFRS.

It is mandatory for holding companies incorporated in Pakistan that have subsidiaries to prepare consolidated financial statements in accordance with requirements of the IFRS for which notification has been issued by SECP.

C. Insurance Ordinance of 2000

The Insurance Ordinance of 2000 regulates the financial reporting practices of insurance companies operating in Pakistan. The ordinance empowers SECP to monitor and enforce the applicable laws and standards, including accounting and auditing for the insurance companies. The financial statements of all insurance companies must be audited by chartered accountants (ICAP members). The auditor is appointed from a SECP-approved panel. The audited financial statements of insurance companies should be submitted to SECP within four months of the end of the financial year. As per the Insurance Ordinance, insurance companies are required to obtain actuarial certification that their reserves adequately meet all obligations to their respective policyholders.

D. Non-banking financial companies department of SECP

The non-banking financial companies (NBFC) department of SECP regulates the non-banking financial institutions in Pakistan, including their accounting and reporting. This department is responsible for regulating investment banks, leasing companies, discount houses, housing finance companies and venture capital companies.

The enforcement and monitoring department of SECP is responsible for enforcing IFRS compliance, investigation, compliance with relevant laws and regulations by listed companies, and for prosecution (except in relation to specialized companies and insurance companies for which SECP has specialized enforcement branches).

Listed companies are required to comply with SECP requirements with respect to financial reporting and disclosures. Pursuant to the authority granted under the Companies Ordinance (sect. 234 (3)), SECP issues special regulatory orders prescribing mandatory IFRS application to listed companies.

The enforcement and monitoring department monitors compliance with IFRS through regular review of the annual and quarterly financial statements published and filed with SECP by listed companies, NBFC and insurance companies. On identifying any disclosure deficiencies or other non-compliance of IFRS, the enforcement and monitoring department imposes fines and penalties on the preparers and their auditors. Over the last few years, the enforcement and monitoring department has penalized several companies, including nearly 25 firms of auditors. Furthermore, the enforcement and monitoring department also refers the cases of defaulting auditors to ICAP for further disciplinary action through its investigation committee.

The NBFC Department of SECP is authorized to monitor and enforce the accounting and auditing requirements for non-banking financial institutions as set by the non-banking finance company rules (2003). The financial statements of the non-banking financial institutions must be audited by the ICAP members.

The insurance division of SECP is empowered to monitor and enforce the applicable laws and standards, including the accounting rules and regulations for the insurance companies.

E. State Bank of Pakistan

The State Bank of Pakistan is the central bank of Pakistan. While its constitution, as originally stated in the State Bank of Pakistan Order of 1948, remained basically unchanged until 1 January 1974, the scope of its functions was considerably enlarged when the banks were nationalized. The State Bank of Pakistan Act of 1956, with subsequent amendments, forms the basis of its operations today.

Currently, over 50 financial institutions are supervised by the State Bank. These include banks, development finance institutions and microfinance banks/institutions. Banks operating in the country include public and private sector banks incorporated in Pakistan and branches of foreign banks.

F. Banking Companies Ordinance of 1962 and the role of the State Bank in the monitoring and enforcement of standards

The Banking Companies Ordinance empowers the State Bank to regulate and supervise commercial banks and financial institutions, including financial reporting by such institutions. The accounting and auditing requirements as outlined in the Banking Companies Ordinance are additional to the requirements contained in the Companies Ordinance. The State Bank has prescribed formats for financial statements, including disclosure requirements that each bank must follow. Due to the exemption granted to financial institutions from the applicability of IAS 39 and IAS 40, these formats deviate from full compliance with IFRS. All banks and development finance institutions must publish audited annual financial statements and file those statements with the State Bank. The financial statements of all banks and development finance institutions must be audited by firms of chartered accountants whose names are included in the panel/list of qualified auditors maintained by the State Bank. Exercising the authority conferred by section 35 (3) of the Banking Companies Ordinance, the State Bank issues guidelines for the auditors, primarily for the purpose of prudential regulations. Bank auditors are required to hold meetings with bank inspectors before commencement of their on-site inspection. In addition, inspectors are required to share their concerns with the respective auditors upon completion of the inspection. Furthermore, the auditors are required to send to the State Bank copies of the management letter and any other letters to bank management within one week of issuance of such letters.

The banking inspection department is one of the core departments of the State Bank. Its mission is to strive for soundness and stability of the financial system and to safeguard interest of stakeholders through proactive inspection, compatible with best international practices.

In order to assess a financial institution, the department conducts regular on-site inspection of all scheduled banks inclusive of foreign banks and development finance institutions. The regular on-site inspection is conducted on the basis of the CAMELS (capital, asset quality, management, earnings, liquidity, sensitivity and system and controls) framework. CAMELS is an effective rating system for evaluating the soundness of financial institutions on a uniform basis and for identifying those institutions requiring special attention or concern. The focus of inspection is generally on risk-assessment policies, and procedures of the banks and control environment to keep attached risks within acceptable limits and in compliance with laws, regulations and supervisory directives. As a further step in the inspection process, discussions are held with external auditors to review banks' internal controls, compliance with legislation, prudential standards and adequacy of provisions. The department works in close coordination with the off-site surveillance desk in the banking supervision department and other departments in SBP.

The off-site supervision and enforcement department is one of the newly created departments emerging in the wake of the reorganization of the former banking supervision department. The new department is responsible for off-site supervision of the financial institutions coming under regulatory purview of the State Bank. The department also ensures effective enforcement of regulatory and supervisory policies, monitors risk profiles, evaluates operating performance of individual banks/development finance institutions and takes necessary enforcement actions against institutions for their non-compliance with laws and regulations put in place by the State Bank, as identified by the inspection teams of the banking inspection department during their on-site examinations, and/or by the supervisors of the off-site supervision and enforcement department based on submitted returns, interaction with financial institutions and market information.

In recent years, the State Bank has inducted a number of chartered accountants and other professionals to strengthen its oversight of financial reporting by banks and other institutions. The bank also works very closely with ICAP and seeks its input/advice on accounting and auditing matters.

G. Institute of Chartered of Accountants of Pakistan

ICAP is an autonomous statutory body established under the Chartered Accountants Ordinance of 1961. It is governed by a 16-member council that includes 12 elected members and 4 members nominated by the Federal Government. The government nominees include the Chairman of SECP, Chairman of the Federal Board of Revenue, Chairman of the National Tariff Commission and the Federal Secretary Privatization Commission. Under the ordinance, the basic duty of ICAP is to regulate the profession of accountants. In order to discharge that duty, which also covers ensuring reliable financial reporting by corporate entities, ICAP has been working together with government agencies and regulators such as SECP and the State Bank. For this purpose, joint ICAP-SECP committees have been established that usually meet on a quarterly basis.

ICAP is an active member of international and regional organizations, such as IFAC, the Confederation of Asian and Pacific Accountants and the South Asian Federation of Accountants.

While ICAP has established robust regulatory mechanisms, the Government of Pakistan, on the recommendation of the ICAP council, has agreed to make necessary amendments in the Charted Accountants Ordinance to further empower the council and to strengthen its disciplinary and regulatory processes

ICAP acts both as an examining body for awarding chartered accountancy qualifications and the licensing and disciplinary authority for members engaged in public practice. ICAP's aggregate membership in July 2006 was 3,864, of which about 15 per cent is engaged in public practice.

H. ICAP's enforcement role as a regulator of the accountancy profession

Members of ICAP are required to follow the ICAP Code of Ethics for Chartered Accountants, which was revised in 2003 in line with the IFAC Code of Ethics for Professional Accountants issued in November 2001. ICAP is currently deliberating adoption of the revised IFAC Code of Ethics issued in June 2005.

Members of ICAP are required to ensure compliance with IFRS: the ICAP council's directive TR 5 requires its members who are auditors of the companies to ensure that the financial statements they audit comply with the requirements of IFRS (except IAS 29 and IFRS 1, 4, 7 and 8, which are under consideration by ICAP).

The Charted Accountants Ordinance has prescribed a procedure to deal with any breach of professional ethics and other instances of misconduct by the members. The Directorate of Corporate Affairs and Investigation works in conjunction with the ICAP investigation committee to investigate such breaches. Under the ordinance, all complaints of misconduct against members of ICAP must be investigated by the investigation committee, which reports to the council for final decision.

During 2007, 20 cases were referred to the investigation committee and 10 cases were concluded as follows:

Closed	3
Members reprimanded by name	2
Reprimanded by name + penalty PRs 1000	1
Members reprimanded without name	2
Members cautioned	0
Membership suspended for six months	1
Reference made to High Court (for termination of membership above five years period)	1
Total	**10**

ICAP has the authority to penalize, reprimand or terminate the membership of the member who is found guilty of misconduct or negligent in performing his or her professional duties. The nature of the penalty depends on the nature and extent of misconduct by members.

I. Quality control review

The directorate of professional standards compliance and evaluation of ICAP carries out the quality control reviews of practising firms that conduct audit of companies. The Quality Assurance Board monitors the ICAP quality control review programme, under which it examines audit working papers and highlights non-compliance with ISAs/IAS, etc., for the auditors concerned. If major departures or non-compliances are observed, then the case is forwarded to the investigation committee for further action against the member.

Quality control reviews of practising firms are carried out for two reasons. The primary reason is to determine whether a practising firm has a satisfactory quality control review rating (which is determined according to assessment of whether or not the audit work was done in accordance with ISAs) to enable it to carry out audits of the listed companies. The second reason is ICAP's desire to help and guide practising firms that are not able to obtain satisfactory rating to develop an appropriate knowledge and skills base so that they can achieve the requisite standard.

J. Quality Assurance Board

The Quality Assurance Board of ICAP was formed in September 2005 to replace the Quality Control Committee, which used to monitor the quality assurance programme of. The board consists of various stakeholders, including representatives from SECP, the State Bank, the Central Board of Revenue and the Karachi Stock Exchange. The chairman of the board is a non-practising chartered accountant.

The Quality Assurance Board suggested revision of the quality control reviews framework, which suggestion was approved by the council on 12 September 2006. The salient features of the revised framework are as follows:

(a) Quality control review of a practising firm will now be carried out after two and a half years instead of two years.

(b) A quality control review must cover at least 25 per cent of audit partners of a practicing firm.

(c) The Quality Assurance Board report will be issued on a whole firm (instead of branch).

(d) Additional files will be reviewed where one file is assessed to be "not-in-accordance" with ISAs applicable in Pakistan.

(e) Files will be shortlisted before the review has ended.

The Quality Assurance Board is currently in the process of incorporating International Standard on Quality Control 1 into the quality control review programme of ICAP, taking into account the practical difficulties of small and medium practices.

III. Capacity-building: The role of the Institute of Charted Accountants of Pakistan in creating awareness of international financial reporting standards

A. Facilitating regulators

ICAP, at the request of regulators, holds separate seminars, workshops on IFRS and ISAs for their teams, i.e., the Federal Board of Revenue, SECP, the State Bank, etc..

These programmes have in fact resulted in bridging of the perception gap between ICAP and the regulators, and have helped develop better understanding of standards by the regulators, leading to smooth implementation and handling of IFRS-related issues.

B. Guidance

ICAP was closely monitoring changes in the IFRS and ISAs, and conducting seminars and workshops whenever a new IFRS or ISA issued by the standard-setters for the guidance of its members. The directorate of technical services of ICAP caters to the needs of the members, especially in practice. The directorate issues guidance in the form of technical releases and circulars for the benefit of the members on local issues. ICAP is not authorized to issue interpretations, which can only be issued by the International Financial Reporting Interpretations Committee.

C. Awareness programmes

Ongoing awareness programmes covering almost all topics have been organized by ICAP to improve the degree of compliance with IFRS requirements. At the first South Asian

Accounting Summit organized by ICAP, prominent scholars from widely recognized bodies such as the IASB were invited to address different issues faced by the accounting profession globally and particularly in the context of Pakistan.

D. Members' information and education series

Considering the needs of its members, especially those in industry, ICAP has launched a series of publications called the *Members Information and Education Series*. This initiative has been very much appreciated by the members.

E. Disclosure checklist

ICAP also develops financial statement disclosure checklists to help preparers and auditors achieve compliance with disclosure requirements of IFRS and local regulatory requirements. The checklist seeks to provide guidance to reporting companies and their auditors with regard to the disclosures to be made in the financial statements prepared in accordance with the approved accounting standards (IFRS, notification of which has been issued by SECP) and the requirements of the Companies Ordinance.

F. Training workshops for small and medium practices

In the year 2006, ICAP initiated a series of training workshops for the students of small and medium practices. The response from small and medium practices was overwhelming and it was encouraging to note that they are keen to improve their procedures and practices, and have made efforts to bring them in line with ISAs issued by the International Assurance and Auditing Standards Board.

ICAP plans to continue such training programmes on a monthly basis all over Pakistan. It is hoped that these workshops will add value to the quality of audits and bring about a positive change in working of various practicing firms.

G. Capacity-building measures

Capacity-building is imperative in consolidating the prior achievements, improving the knowledge base among auditors and the preparers of financial statements and strengthening the monitoring and enforcement mechanisms for ensuring compliance with applicable standards and codes. This includes improving the capacity of regulators and professional bodies, upgrading accountancy education and training with focus on practical application of IFRS and ISAs, issuing and disseminating implementation guidance on applicable standards, developing simplified SME reporting requirements, upgrading the licensing procedure for professional accountants and auditors and enhancing the delivery of continuing professional education.

H. Capacity-building at ICAP

ICAP is committed to IFAC's seven statements of membership obligations. In fact, the council has carried out a gap analysis with a view to achieving full compliance with such statements in the near future. While ICAP played an effective leadership role in the past for adoption and implementation of international accounting and auditing standards, it continues to work on further enhancing its capacity to fulfil its responsibility in the public interest of regulating the accounting profession in line with international best practices. ICAP has also proved itself to be an active member of IFAC, the South Asian Federation of Accountants and the Confederation of Asian and Pacific Accountants, and participated actively in international events. The ICAP governance structure is also considered to be in line with the best practices followed by other international bodies. Furthermore, in recent years, ICAP has substantially increased the number of qualified people in its different departments. For example, it has increased the number of charted accountants employed by ICAP to 25, as compared with 17 in 2005.

I. Upgrading the licensing procedure of professional accountants and auditors

ICAP is working towards upgrading the licensing procedure of professional accountants and auditors. This involves changing the by-laws to introduce more stringent licensing and renewal requirements and strengthening practical training aspects.

Audit of listed companies is only performed by the firm having a satisfactory quality control review rating. Under the review framework, every firm of chartered accountants performing audit of listed companies is required to obtain a satisfactory rating at least once every two and half years.

New training regulations have been introduced to strengthen practical training aspects. These regulations cover the requirements as stipulated in the international education standard (IES) 5 on practical experience requirement.

ICAP is currently developing guidelines for networking of audit firms. This will help small and medium-sized practices to enhance their resources, thus improving the quality of audits.

J. Enhancing the delivery of continuing professional education

The Continuing Professional Development Programme of ICAP is already in place and aims to keep ICAP members abreast of the changes in the international accounting and auditing standards and other relevant subjects. The programme is in line with IES 7, and continuing professional development committees and regional committees organize seminars and workshops on IFRS, ISAs and relevant local pronouncements on a regular basis. Members are required to attend a minimum number of 40 hours of such seminars and workshops during the year. The programme is to be further strengthened and made available across the country.

To achieve this goal, ICAP organized the first South Asian Accounting Summit in 2006, which brought together senior representatives from the global standards setters, including the chairman of the IASB, Sir David Tweedie, office-bearers of the major accounting bodies in the South Asian region and leading accounting professionals of the country.

K. Developing simplified SME reporting tools

ICAP aspires to extend practical assistance to SMEs in implementing SME standards for which it is developing illustrative financial statements and disclosure checklists.

L. Adoption of interpretations issued by IFRIC

All interpretations on IAS/IFRS that are issued by IFRIC (or its predecessor body, the Standing Interpretations Committee) are considered as adopted. ICAP does not formally adopt any of the interpretations issued by IFRIC for the reason that interpretations (issued by the Standing Interpretations Committee or IFRIC) always relate to a particular standard (IAS/IFRS) and are presumed to be automatically adopted with the adoption of the relevant standard as are revisions to standards.

M. Training regulations

Training regulations have been implemented with effect from April 2006. This will further strengthen various aspects of gaining practical experience. These regulations generally cover the requirements as stipulated in IES 5 on practical experience requirement, issued by

IFAC to ensure that future members acquire skills and values necessary for responding to the dynamics of the profession.

N. Board of Studies

In 2006, ICAP re-established the Board of Studies to be headed by a full-time chairman. The board shall, for example, conduct educational research and development, prepare description of courses and develop syllabi and course outlines, identify books for recommended reading and develop study material.

An advisory committee with members from various professional fields and various stakeholders has been constituted to advise the Board of Studies on various matters.

O. Pakistan Accounting Research Foundation

In March 2006, the ICAP council approved in principle the formation of the trust Pakistan Accounting Research Foundation. The trust has been established for education, research and development of the accounting profession and allied services, and shall exist on a non-profit basis. The primary functions of foundation include:

(a) Forming a state-of-the-art university of accounting and finance;

(b) Providing assistance including financial and professional support to persons involved in research and development;

(c) Making endeavours to improve the standards of the accountancy profession;

(d) Arranging coordination between local and foreign students; and

(e) Arranging bilateral exchange of information, etc.

IV. Lessons learned

In Pakistan, the regulators of the corporate and financial sectors and ICAP, which represent the accounting profession, are of the firm view that financial reporting by public interest entities should be in conformity with the international financial reporting standards so as to generate high-quality financial information that is relevant, comparable, consistent and transparent and thus serving the needs of stakeholders. In this regard, ICAP's proactive leadership of the profession and collaborative approach of working together with the regulators has helped bring about significant improvement in the quality of financial reporting in line with international standards. Further, ICAP's strategy of adopting IFRS over the last two decades, rather than adaptation, has also helped promote acceptance and understanding of and compliance with IFRS among preparers and users of the financial statements. The process involved overcoming challenges which included limitations of technical resources, capacity issues, coordination and effective advocacy with the regulators, to ensure smooth implementation of IFRS in the country. The major lessons learned during the process are discussed below.

A. Verbatim adoption of international financial reporting standards

From the very beginning, ICAP followed the approach of verbatim adoption of IAS/IFRS instead of making changes to the text of standards to bring them in line with the local regulatory and business environment. The approach has been to bring the regulatory requirements in line with IFRS rather than the contrary. While this approach involved considerable difficulties at the initial adoption and implementation stage for which ICAP faced criticism, sometimes from its own members, in the long run this approach has served the interest of the profession and the country, as most people now agree that Pakistan has been able to develop high-quality financial reporting as a result of this approach. In addition, Pakistan will be able to achieve full IFRS compliance in the next two or three years without too much difficulty.

B. Keeping up-to-date with revisions/conforming amendments to IFRS

Revisions and conforming amendments to IAS/IFRS by the International Accounting Standards Board are a regular feature now, and keeping track of whether the individual revision/amendment has been adopted and notification issued has become all the more challenging.

As a strategy, ICAP decided that once a standard is adopted by ICAP and notified by SECP, any subsequent revision/conforming amendment made by the board is considered as adopted unless otherwise specified.

This strategy has helped Pakistan keep up-to-date with the latest developments in the standards which otherwise, with the limited availability of technical resources, would have become extremely difficult.

C. Implementation of certain requirements of international financial reporting standards – a gradual process

Adopting IFRS is not just an accounting exercise, but also is a transition that requires participation and support of all stakeholders, including preparers, auditors and users. When adopting and implementing IFRS, it should not be forgotten that, in certain cases, it may cause undue hardship to the industry, at least in the beginning. For example, the Pakistani banking industry was not prepared to apply the provisions of IAS 39 immediately because of capacity and other related issues discussed earlier. Transitory measures had to be adopted, including providing adequate time for gradual implementation.

D. Working together with the regulators

Since its inception, ICAP has played a key role in adoption of, creating awareness of, education on and implementation of IFRS. A major factor in achieving this success was the collaborative approach adopted by ICAP of working together with the main corporate and financial regulators in public interest.

E. Addressing differences between international financial reporting standards and law

As a recommending authority of financial reporting standards, ICAP has learned that where the accounting treatments prescribed in various IFRS are in conflict with the corresponding legal requirements, its role has become all the more important, acting in the best interest of the country and stakeholders at large, as well as balancing its responsibilities as a signatory to the membership obligations of IFAC. The approach adopted to deal with such issues varied with the nature and magnitude of the issue.

1. Changes in law as per the accounting requirements

Since most of the commercial and corporate laws of the country have evolved from statutes drafted several decades ago, in most cases, such laws are not consistent with the financial reporting needs of the corporate sector. Consequently, ICAP has in most cases worked to persuade government officials and regulators of the need to make amendments to bring them in conformity with international standards.

2. Making a particular accounting requirement inapplicable to a sector of the economy

While in most cases laws and regulations are modified to make them consistent with IFRS, in certain cases, immediate application of IFRS would be counterproductive, so ICAP has adopted a more pragmatic approach of either allowing more time or providing exemption to certain sectors. For instance, in the case of IAS 39, ICAP supported the banking sector's demand for more time and deferral of the standard for a considerable period. Similarly, in view of the genuine difficulties faced by the independent power producers on account of interpretation No. 4 of International Financial Reporting Interpretations Committee, which would have converted all of these entities into leasing companies, ICAP supported the deferral of interpretation No. 4 up to 2009.

F. IFRS are not made to fit all entity sizes

ICAP realized that mandatory application of all IFRS to all companies is not practical and separate standards must be developed for SMEs before embarking on full IFRS compliance regime in the country.

Given the substantial increase and complexities of IFRS, it is not possible for SMEs to ensure full compliance with all their requirements. In reality, these SMEs lack adequate technical capabilities and resources to ensure compliance with complicated reporting requirements. Consequently, ICAP took the initiative of developing two separate financial reporting standards for SMEs, which are expected to be notified by SECP soon.

G. Involvement of stakeholders in the adoption and implementation process

In order to create awareness and ensure stakeholder participation, ICAP has been holding seminars, roundtables and workshops to get sufficient support from the stakeholders in the process of adoption and implementation of IFRS. This approach is considered essential for effective implementation.

H. Role of the Quality Assurance Board in improving standards of auditing and financial reporting

The quality control review programme, in addition to ensuring compliance with the standards, is also educative in nature. Over the years, effective and regular quality assurance reviews conducted by ICAP's professional standards compliance department under the supervision of the Quality Assurance Board (previously the Quality Control Committee) have helped in bringing about sustained improvements in the audit quality and compliance with IFRS.

I. Investment in training and education in international financial reporting standards

An extensive and effective training and education programme is considered imperative for proper understanding and implementation of IFRS. More specifically, some of the complex accounting standards – such as IAS 39, IAS 36, etc. – require significant training and education for proper understanding and implementation. While ICAP has been pursuing a continuing education programme for its members and other stakeholders, there is a need for further investment in this area.

With the issuance of newer accounting standards or revision of existing ones on the basis of IFRS, various new concepts are being introduced (e.g. fair value concept), on which the preparers, auditors, analysts and other users need to be adequately trained and educated.

V. Conclusions

With all three factors – i.e. implementation, regulatory framework and quality assurance – moving in the right direction, Pakistan is on track for and rapidly approaching full IFRS compliance in the next two or three years, in line with the IFRS strategy approved by the ICAP council.

The target date for achieving full IFRS compliance is December 2009, so the financial statements prepared in Pakistan for the periods beginning on or after 1 January 2010 should be IFRS-compliant allowing all publicly accountable entities are able to give an unreserved compliance with IFRS.

The ICAP quality control review programme is committed to a process of continuous and sustained improvement. The ultimate objective of this very important regulatory and educative programme is to maintain and enhance the reputation and image of this prestigious profession.

Chapter VIII

Case study of South Africa

I. Introduction[1]

South Africa is regarded as the economic powerhouse of Africa, with a gross domestic product (GDP) four times that of its southern African neighbours and comprising around 25 per cent of the entire continent's GDP.[2] This positive picture of the South African economy is confirmed in the Chairman and Chief Executive Officer Statement of the Johannesburg Stock Exchange (JSE):

"The South African economy continues its strong performance, and translates into increased interest in the market from local and international investors, and trading volumes reach record levels...The building blocks for this success have been put in place by Government, and we must applaud its efforts in creating an environment in which the economy can thrive. A continued commitment to prudent macroeconomic policies builds confidence in South Africa as an investment destination, and boosts the image of the country as a whole. The JSE plays its role in providing an efficient, well-regulated exchange that makes the investment process as simple, low cost and transparent as possible, but the underlying investment decision is dependent upon perceptions of the future performance of South Africa as a whole."[3]

The Minister of Finance, Trevor Manual, in summarizing the Government's efforts in the budget speech of 2007, said:

"As our young nation enters its thirteenth year, we have much to be proud of. We are building a society founded on principles of equality, non-racialism and non-sexism. We have built institutions of democracy, creating an open society founded on a rule of law. After stabilizing the economy and the public finance, we have created the conditions for rapid economic growth, job creation and the broadening of opportunities."[4]

The South African Institute of Chartered Accountants (SAICA), the JSE and the Accounting Practices Board (APB) of South Africa have recognized the need to be part of a global economy with respect to financial reporting.[5] Local accounting standards in South Africa have been harmonized with international accounting standards since 1993.[6] In February 2004, a decision was taken by the APB to issue the text of international financial reporting standards

---

[1] This document was prepared and edited by the UNCTAD secretariat with substantive inputs from the South African Institute of Chartered Accountants (SAICA).

[2] Available from www.southafrica.info/business/economy/econoverview.htm (accessed 25 June 2007).

[3] JSE: Chairman and CEO Statement. Available from www.jse.co.za/chairmanceo.jsp (accessed 25 June 2007).

[4] South African Government (2007). Budget Speech 2007 by Minister of Finance, Trevor Manual, MP. 21 February 2007. Available from www.info.gov.za.

[5] The Accounting Practices Board was established in 1973, the year in which the current Companies Act was enacted.

[6] SAICA (2004). Preface to Statements of Generally Accepted Accounting Practice. August 2004. SAICA (2006). Circular 03/06 – Evaluation of Compliance with Statements of Generally Accepted Accounting Practice. March 2006.

(IFRS) as South African statements of generally accepted accounting practice (GAAP) without any amendments.[7] The reasons for the ongoing harmonizing and the issuing of the text of IFRS as South African statements of GAAP were:

(a) "For South African companies to attract foreign investment;

(b) To provide credibility to the financial statements of South African companies in the global market; and

(c) To do away with the need for dual listed entities to prepare financial statements in accordance with more than one set of accounting standards."[8]

The main purpose of this case study is to set out South Africa's experience in the implementation of IFRS.[9] The case study starts in chapter II by providing a brief overview of the current financial reporting system in South Africa, including the development of the system and proposed reforms. The transition to IFRS in South Africa is integrated into this discussion. Thereafter, the South African experience in converting South African standards into IFRS is discussed, with a focus on issues of a more general nature (chapter III), and specific technical and application issues are presented in chapter IV.

II.   The South African financial reporting system

The legal framework for corporate reporting in South Africa is governed by the 1973 Companies Act (No. 61). However, the standard-setting process (discussed below) is developed in South Africa outside the scope of the Companies Act.

A. Companies Act

The 1973 Companies Act requires that the financial statements of companies be in conformity with generally accepted accounting practice.[10] The concept of statements of GAAP was introduced into the Companies Act with the introduction of paragraph 5 into schedule 4 to the Act in 1992.[11] It stated that if the directors of a company believe that there are reasons for departing from any of the accounting concepts in the statements of GAAP approved by the APB in preparing the company's financial statements in respect of any accounting period, they may do so, but particulars of the departure, the effects and the reasons for it shall be given.

Legal opinion was obtained by SAICA in September 1999 to interpret the effect of these provisions of the Companies Act.[12] The opinion merely confirmed that, to meet the requirements of the Companies Act, the financial statements should be prepared and presented in accordance with generally accepted accounting practice. However, the required disclosure needed to be provided if the financial statements materially departed from statements of GAAP. Only

---

[7] Ibid.

[8] Ludolph S (2006). Why IFRS? Accounting SA. April: 19. (Sue Ludolph is the SAICA Project Director – Accounting).

[9] Except for different documents referred to in this report, the South African experience is obtained from discussions with representatives of companies such as Telkom, Sasol, the JSE and the Standard Bank, and the auditors, Deloitte.

[10] South Africa (1973). Companies Act No. 61 of 1973, sect. 283(6). Pretoria: Government Printer.

[11] SAICA (2005). Circular 8/99 – Compliance with sect. 286(3) and para. 5 of schedule 4 to Companies Act No. 61 of 1973 and statements of generally accepted accounting practice. June 1999.

[12] Ibid.

additional disclosure was required. A no true and fair view override, similar to IAS 1 (presentation of financial statements), was created by the Companies Act.

The result is that the current Companies Act does not require companies to comply with South African statements of GAAP. Thus, no statutory enforcement procedures for statements of GAAP have been created by the Companies Act.

B. The standard-setting process in South Africa

Standard-setting in South Africa follows a two-level process. While the APB approves and issues accounting standards, the Accounting Practices Committee serves as an advisory body to the APB.

The objective of the Accounting Practices Committee in this regard is firstly to propose to the APB the issuing in South Africa of the international statements of GAAP (AC 100 series) and interpretations of statements of GAAP (AC 400 series).[13] A second objective of the committee is to develop South African pronouncements of statements of GAAP and interpretation (AC 500 series) in instances where issues are relevant to the South African context only. The AC 500 series developed by the committee also undergoes a process of exposure and review of comments before being recommended to the APB.

An exposure draft of a proposed IFRS, issued by the International Accounting Standards Board (IASB), is issued for comment by the committee at the same time and for a period similar to the IASB in South Africa.[14] Comments received on the South African version of the exposure draft are considered by the committee in its process of drafting the comment letter submitted by SAICA to the IASB. Once the IASB issues an IFRS, the committee reviews the IFRS to ensure that it is not in conflict with any South African legislation before recommending to the APB that it is issued as a South African statement of GAAP.

Since 1993, as stated above, South Africa has been harmonizing its statements of GAAP with international standards, even though the South African versions of the international standards have been issued as South African statements of GAAP (AC 100 series) and interpretation of statements of GAAP (AC 400 series) after a due process. As a result, South African statements of GAAP have been, in most respects, similar to IFRS. Minor differences have arisen as a result of different effective dates, and, in some instances, options permitted in IFRS have been removed from South African statements of GAAP and additional disclosure requirements have been included.[15]

In February 2004, the APB decided to issue the text of IFRS as South African statements of GAAP without any amendments (see above). From then on, each South African statement of GAAP would be identical to each IFRS. However, transitional differences, such as implementation dates, could still exist, since a South African due process is still followed. To indicate the similarity between each IFRS and its corresponding South African statement of GAAP, a dual numbering system is used to refer to both the IFRS number and the relevant statement of GAAP number in the South African statements of GAAP.[16]

If an entity applies South African statements of GAAP, it cannot claim compliance with IFRS because of the transitional differences that still exist.

---

[13] SAICA (2004). Preface to Statement of Generally Accepted Accounting Practice. August 2004.
[14] Ibid.
[15] SAICA (2006). Circular 03/06 – Evaluation of Compliance with Statements of Generally Accepted Accounting Practice. March 2006.
[16] Ibid.

In respect to the public sector, statements of generally recognized accounting practice (GRAP) are issued by the APB in South Africa.[17] A key priority of the APB is to develop a core set of standards of GRAP by 2009. These statements of GRAP are drawn primarily from the International Public Sector Accounting Standards issued by the International Public Sector Accounting Standards Board of the International Federation of Accountants.

C. JSE Limited

The Johannesburg Stock Exchange (JSE) was originally established as the Johannesburg Stock Exchange in 1887. The name changed to JSE Securities Exchange South Africa on 8 November 2000, when it became a national exchange and expanded to other financial products. In 2005, JSE revised its corporate identity and changed its name to JSE Limited.[18]

JSE is among the 20 largest stock exchanges in the world and provides capital to large listed entities, with its alternative exchange offering access for small businesses, and its social responsibility index supporting businesses that invest in socially, economically, and environmentally sustainable development. As of the week ended 22 June 2007, the JSE market capitalization was 5.814 billion rands, an increase of 40.9 per cent from the corresponding week in 2006.[19]

Currently, just over 50 companies with dual listings are registered on JSE, of which more than half are primarily listed in South Africa.[20] This demonstrates that most of these companies originated in South Africa. However, some companies with dual listings, such as SABMiller and BHP Billiton, have been created through international mergers and takeovers. Only five of these companies are listed on the New York Stock Exchange and will benefit if the United States GAAP reconciliation is abolished.

As of October 2000, JSE required listed companies to prepare their annual financial statements in accordance with the national law applicable to listed companies (the Companies Act) and to apply either South African statements of GAAP or International Accounting Standards.[21] The reason for allowing the choice was to assist companies with dual listings on overseas stock exchanges and overseas companies listed on JSE.

Further revised listing requirements called for listed companies to comply with IFRS for financial periods commencing on or after 1 January 2005.[22] In the light of the above, the APC took a decision to issue the text of IFRS in South Africa without any amendments in February 2004.[23]

D. Developed practice

Although the Companies Act does not explicitly require companies to apply South African GAAP, such a practice has developed in South Africa. This practice is also confirmed by

---

[17] Statements of GRAP are available at www.asb.co.za

[18] JSE (2007). Our history. Available from www.jse.co.za/our_history.jsp (accessed 23 April 2007).

[19] JSE (2007). Weekly Statistics: Week ended 22 June 2007.

[20] JSE (2007). Dual Listed Company Information. Available from www.jse.co.za (accessed 25 June 2006).

[21] Section 8.62(b) of the then JSE listing requirements.

[22] Section 8.3 of the JSE limited listing requirements.

[23] SAICA (2006). Circular 03/06 – Evaluation of Compliance with Statements of Generally Accepted Accounting Practice, March 2006.

the audit practice in South Africa, which does not recognize generally accepted accounting practice as a financial reporting framework for audit assurance purposes.[24]

To confirm this practice, and taking into account the JSE requirements discussed above, SAICA issued a circular in 2006 stating that:[25]

(a)   Companies listed on JSE must prepare financial statements in terms of IFRS, and unlisted companies are permitted to do so.

(b)   Unlisted companies that choose not to follow IFRS must prepare financial statements in terms of South African Statements of GAAP. Where there is a departure from such statements, the departure, its particulars, the reason for the departure and its effect on the financial statements must be disclosed.

(c)   If unlisted companies choose to adopt IFRS by way of an explicit and unreserved statement of compliance with IFRS, IFRS 1 must be applied in the preparation of their first set of IFRS financial statements. Unlisted companies that comply with statements of GAAP are not permitted to use the IFRS 1 (AC 138) [26] option.

This circular issued by SAICA does not create any regulating authority on unlisted companies. It is foreseen that corporate law reform will legislate this practice in South Africa. Further, no relief is currently available for small and medium-sized enterprises (SMEs) in South Africa.

E. Corporate Law Amendment Act

The Corporate Law Amendment Act 2006 was issued on 17 April 2007 as the first official document in the process of the reform of the Companies Act, but at the time of writing (July 2007) does not have an effective date. It has been seen as the first phase of the reform process. The second phase entails a complete review of the Companies Act.[27]

The Corporate Law Amendment Act provides for differential accounting in South Africa by identifying two types of companies: a widely held company and a limited interest company. The Amendment Act specifically declares that financial reporting standards for widely held companies shall be in accordance with IFRS.[28] A company will be classified as widely held if its articles provide for unrestricted transfer of its shares, if it is permitted by its articles (or by special resolution) to offer shares to the public, or if it is a subsidiary of a widely held company.

Once the Corporate Law Amendment Act is effective, relief will be granted to limited interest companies in that they will not have to comply with the stringent requirements of IFRS or South African Statements of GAAP. However, the financial reporting standards for limited interest companies still need to be developed. As an interim measure, limited interest companies are required to prepare their financial statements in terms of accounting policies adopted, which must comply with the framework for the preparation and presentation of financial statements (AC

---

[24] Public Accountants and Auditors Board (2005). South African Auditing Practice Statement (SAAPS 2) – Financial reporting frameworks and audit opinions. July 2005.

[25] SAICA (2006). Circular 03/06 – Evaluation of Compliance with Statements of Generally Accepted Accounting Practice. March 2006.

[26] SAICA (2006). IFRS 1 (AC 138) – First-time Adoption of International Financial Reporting Standards, the South African equivalent to IFRS 1.

[27] SAICA (2007). Summary of the main features of the Corporate Laws Amendment Bill. Johannesburg: SAICA.

[28] Sect. 440S(2) of the Corporate Law Amendment Act 2006.

000 in the South African context, which is identical to the IASB conceptual framework).[29] In anticipation of this relief for limited interest companies, the Accounting Practices Committee will recommend to the APB an early adoption of IASB ED 222 (IFRS for SMEs) as a transitional measure.[30]

A further initiative of the Corporate Law Amendment Act is the establishment of the statutory Financial Reporting Standards Council (FRSC), which will take over the function of the APB as the non-statutory standard setter in South Africa. Until the FRSC is established, the APB will continue its function as the South African standard-setting body. The objective of the FRSC will be to establish financial reporting standards that promote sound and consistent accounting practices.[31] The functions of the FRSC will be to:

(a) Establish financial reporting standards for widely held companies in accordance with IFRS; and

(b) Develop separate reporting standards for SMEs in South Africa.[32]

F. Enforcement

Currently, the Companies Act does not create any procedures for the enforcement of financial reporting in South Africa.

As an interim phase, in 2002 JSE, in partnership with SAICA, established the GAAP Monitoring Panel in response to the need to create an oversight body that would enhance compliance with accounting standards.[33] The results of investigations by the panel are reported to JSE, which takes action against any company guilty of non-compliance. (This is discussed further in chapter III below.)

The Corporate Law Amendment Act also creates initiatives for the monitoring and enforcement of financial reporting standards. For monitoring purposes the Act proposes that a suitably qualified officer may be appointed to monitor the financial reports and accounting practices of certain widely held companies in order to detect non-compliance with financial reporting standards that may prejudice users.[34]

To enhance enforcement, the Corporate Law Amendment Act proposes that the Financial Reporting Investigation Panel be created to replace the GAAP Monitoring Panel. The objective of the new panel will be to contribute to the reliability of financial reports by investigating alleged non-compliance with financial reporting standards and recommending measures for rectification or restitution.[35] Any person, whether or not a shareholder, who has reason to believe that the financial report of a widely held company has failed to comply with a financial reporting standard may refer the matter to the panel for investigation. The Financial Reporting Investigation Panel will have much wider powers than the GAAP Monitoring Panel. Once the Financial Reporting

---

[29] Sect. 56(3) of the fourth schedule of the Corporate Law Amendment Act 2006.
[30] SAICA issued ED 225 – Financial Reporting for Small And Medium-Sized Entities (SMEs) – Proposed Process in May 2007 to invite the South African accounting practice to comment on the process leading to the early adoption of the IFRS for SMEs in South Africa.
[31] Sect. 440P(1) of the Corporate Law Amendment Act 2006.
[32] Sect. 440S(1) of the Corporate Law Amendment Act 2006.
[33] SAICA (2006). GAAP Monitoring Panel has taken a closer look at 30 listed companies. Press release. 29 November 2006.
[34] Sect. 440V of the Corporate Law Amendment Act 2006.
[35] Sect. 440W of the Corporate Law Amendment Act 2006.

Investigation Panel is established and fully operational, it is the intention of SAICA and JSE to dissolve the GAAP Monitoring Panel.[36]

III. Implementation issues of a general nature

The major implementation issues of a general nature encountered in South Africa with the transition to IFRS are discussed in this chapter. Although both SAICA and JSE were instrumental in publicizing the decision to implement IFRS in South Africa (SAICA and JSE communicated the nature of the IFRS implementation decision through press releases and circulars), they were not involved in developing the strategy to implement IFRS. Each company had to adopt its own strategy as is explained below.

A. Transition to IFRS

As stated earlier, JSE required that all listed companies comply with IFRS for financial periods commencing on or after 1 January 2005. Two groups of listed companies existed in South Africa in 2005: those that had already adopted IFRS before 2005 by voluntarily electing to convert, and those that had converted in 2005. Some of the companies in the first group had adopted IFRS before 2005 as they were dual listed on other security exchanges and IFRS was more internationally recognized.

Many companies in South Africa, especially in the banking industry, saw the implementation of IFRS as a two-step process. Firstly, under South African statements of GAAP, the principles of IAS 39 on financial instruments (recognition and measurement) were adopted in 2001/02.[37] Secondly, the full adoption of IFRS occurred in 2005. IFRS 3 on business combinations and the consequent amendments to IAS 36 on impairment to assets and IAS 38 on intangible assets were applicable under South African statements of GAAP from 2004.[38] This could create the impression that transition to IFRS in South Africa during 2005 was not a burdensome process. However, two surveys conducted by Ernst and Young in South Africa demonstrated that South Africa's transition to IFRS in 2005 was still a significant and costly exercise for most companies.

Ernst and Young carried out a survey of 46 JSE-listed companies in the first quarter of 2005 to investigate the IFRS implementation status of companies in South Africa.[39] The survey indicated that 96 per cent of the companies surveyed were not on track for reporting IFRS 2005 interim results and that only 33 per cent were on track with the overall progress of the IFRS 2005 implementation. This clearly indicates that many South African companies underestimated the transition to IFRS.

In 2006, Ernst and Young conducted a follow-up survey to assess the implications and impact of the IFRS transition both for first-time adopters (IFRS conversion) and previous adopters (the effect of the improvements project).[40] The survey highlighted the challenges South African companies faced with the adoption of IFRS, which included greater complexity than

---

[36] SAICA (2007). Summary of the main features of the Corporate Law Amendment Bill. Johannesburg: SAICA.

[37] AC 133, the South African equivalent of IAS 39, was applicable for financial years starting from 1 January 2001.

[38] IFRS 3 (AC 140) – Business Combinations was applicable to all business combinations with an agreement date on or after 31 March 2004.

[39] Ernst and Young (2005). IFRS readiness amongst South African companies – a survey. April 2005.

[40] Ernst and Young (2006). Transition to IFRS – the final analysis results. No date.

anticipated, high costs in some cases, poor understanding of the reasoning behind the transition, and potential confusion about company performance information.[41]

The survey indicated that almost two thirds of the respondents surveyed made use of a steering committee for their IFRS projects and held regular meetings to assess progress and discuss issues. Nearly all of the companies implemented IFRS in house, but over 80 per cent indicated that they were assisted by their external auditors and/or other external consultants (including other auditing firms). What mostly occurred was that the external consultants presented their findings, and the companies' auditors were involved in verifying the choices made and policies implemented by the companies. Consistency and control procedures were created through such a review process.

The transition to IFRS also placed a burden on company staff. Training of staff was deemed necessary and, in response to the survey, approximately a third of the companies indicated that they had had to employ staff on a permanent basis to take responsibility for compliance with accounting standards and disclosure requirements. Some respondents had employed staff from the inception of the IFRS project, while others were still looking for additional staff to assist with the accounting function. In practice, because South Africa was one of the first countries to harmonize its accounting standards with IFRS, its experience is sought after by other countries. Experienced accountants with relevant skills in IFRS are leaving South Africa to work in other countries. This has occurred particularly in relation to the implementation of the financial instrument standards (IAS 32 and 39).

At present, 5,942 of the 26,222 SAICA members (26.6 percent) who hold the South African chartered accountant designation are based outside South Africa.[42] To date, SAICA has focused its attention on the education and training of chartered accountants. SAICA has also identified the need to better assess the supply of and demand for accounting and financial expertise at all levels in South Africa. To understand the nature and extent of the current shortage in financial management, accounting and auditing skills, and nature and extent of the retention of trainee accountants, SAICA launched two research projects during June 2007.[43] These projects are a first step toward resolving the skills shortage in the accounting field in South Africa.

The 2006 survey also indicated enormous cost and time constraints for certain companies in the adoption of IFRS. One third of the respondents had taken more than a year to implement the changes, while only a small group (16 per cent) had taken less than six months. More than half the respondents indicated that the IFRS implementation had cost them more than R1 million and more than 10 per cent believed that the cost had exceeded R5 million.

In the survey, most of the respondents (66 per cent) indicated that the IFRS changes had resulted in more meaningful information being provided to shareholders. However, they also indicated that the adoption of IFRS brought with it increased intricacies and complexities.

Interestingly, the survey pointed to a mixed impact on the bottom-line profit being reported. Almost 66 per cent of the respondents indicated an adverse effect, while approximately one third reported a positive effect.

One of the most significant findings of the survey concerned the impact on the recording and maintenance of financial information. Information and communication technology (ICT)

---

[41] Ernst and Young (2006). Facing the challenges of IFRS adoption. 27 July 2006.

[42] SAICA (2007). CA(SA) qualification results reflect blossoming transformation in accountancy profession. Press release. 22 June 2007.

[43] SAICA (2007). Request for proposal: research into the financial management, accounting and auditing skills shortage, and request for proposal: research into the attrition and retention of trainee accountants.

systems were reported to be unable to supply information in all instances and workarounds were reported to be required to achieve compliance with IFRS, which suggests that more ICT system changes will be seen in the future. Concerns were expressed mostly in the following areas:

(a)   Maintenance of information relating to property, plant and equipment, such as updating of the fixed asset register and recording and updating of the residual values and useful lives: In the transition to IFRS in 2005, the improvements to IAS 16 on property, plant and equipment were seen as the most burdensome task. Many companies applied the deemed cost approach in IFRS 1 to eliminate retrospective adjustments. However, uncertainty about the level of application of the component approach to depreciation remained a challenge.

(b)   Financial-instrument valuation and recording, including risk-management disclosures, complying with de-recognition principles and splitting financial instruments: Currently, under IFRS 7 on financial instruments (disclosure), companies trading in different countries with different functional currencies experience difficulty in completing sensitivity analyses.

(c)   Processes around doubtful debt provisions and accounting for employee and management/executive compensation: The South African experiences surrounding doubtful debt provisions are discussed in greater detail below.

B. Local technical committee

With the adoption of IFRS, the question could be raised whether a local technical committee, such as the South African Accounting Practices Committee, is indeed still needed. The South African experience confirms a need for such a committee.

The first need for such a committee is to achieve the involvement of the local accounting community in the due process of standard setting by the IASB and the International Financial Reporting Interpretations Committee (IFRIC) through commenting on exposure drafts and discussion papers. Firstly, the committee is regarded as being representative of the South African corporate world in that members of the committee represent commerce and industry, users, auditors, JSE and academics. Further, by creating a separate technical subcommittee for each new exposure draft or discussion paper, the committee invites the local accounting community and industry experts to be involved in its comment process should this be necessary.

The second need for such a committee is the role it plays in education. The committee assumes the role of educating the local accounting community on new developments in the accounting field. Road shows (sometimes involving IASB staff) and other opportunities for discussion are held when the need is identified. SAICA, through its continued education process, also provides training seminars to its members on pre-identified topics.

The last, and maybe the most important, need for a committee such as the Accounting Practices Committee is that such a committee should consider the correct treatment of accounting issues for which there is currently insufficient guidance in IFRS, including also instances where diversity in practice is detected. Such issues to be discussed and resolved by the committee are obtained through the following role players:

(a)   The committee members themselves;

(b)   Other SAICA committees;

(c)   Industry committees;

(d)   The technical partners' forum;

(e)   JSE;

(f)   The top 40 chief financial officer forum; and

(g)   Members of SAICA.

C. Local issues and diversity in practice

The experience in South Africa is that diversity exists in practice. However, one of the main advantages of converting to IFRS is that, through this conversion, many of these divergent practices have been eliminated. By adopting IFRS, companies have had to evaluate their existing accounting policies and procedures. The involvement of external consultants and the review process of the internal auditors have created a move toward consistency in implementation. Consistency has been strengthened by industry experts coming together and resolving related issues. In this regard, the technical partners' forum plays a vital role in resolving issues and creating consistency. Each of these technical partners also has the support of their international technical desk.

Local issues and diversity in practice that cannot be resolved through the above structures are channelled to the Accounting Practices Committee. The task of the committee is then to determine the appropriate means of resolving these issues. The first question that the committee asks is whether the issues are widespread and significantly divergent to send a request to IFRIC. Issues such as operating leases and black economic empowerment (BEE) transactions (discussed further in chapter IV below) are examples of South African requests that have been referred to IFRIC.

If the decision is made not to refer an issue to IFRIC for a number of valid reasons (e.g. the issue is considered to be only a local one), the alternatives are to release a local standard, a circular or a guide, or to use other communication methods of announcing how the issue has been resolved. The committee recommends the issuing of such South African pronouncements to the appropriate authoritative body.

Where appropriate, a local standard (one of the AC 500 series of statements of GAAP) is issued by the APB to interpret specific accounting aspects, transactions or other issues that occur only in the South African context, where such aspects, transactions or other issues are not specifically or clearly addressed in IFRS.[44] The AC 500 series has the same authority as the AC 100 series of statements of GAAP, and must be adhered to by South African companies even if they prepare the financial statements in accordance with IFRS.[45] A company which claimed compliance with IFRS and which also complied with the AC 500 series would not be in contravention of IFRS, as these local standards are merely local interpretations of IFRS. These companies would not need to also claim compliance with South African statements of GAAP, and in fact would not be able to as they would have applied IFRS 1 (which is not part of South African statements of GAAP).

The guides issued by SAICA are not regarded as having the same status as statements of GAAP.[46] Members or associates that are responsible for preparing financial statements and that

---

[44] SAICA (2005). Circular 8/05 – Status of Professional Announcements. August 2005.
[45] JSE (2005). Compliance with the AC 500 Series of Standards. JSE listing division's letter. 12 May 2003.
[46] SAICA (2005). Circular 8/05 – Status of Professional Announcements. August 2005.

do not comply with a guide could be called upon by SAICA to explain why they did not do so. Most of the guides are issued to resolve industry-specific issues.

Circulars issued by SAICA communicate relevant issues to members, but never interpret issues. Where communication is provided on accounting issues, circulars have the same status as the accounting guides referred to above.[47]

The more significant of these pronouncements are discussed under specific issues in chapter IV below.

D. Monitoring and enforcement

The formation of the GAAP Monitoring Panel has also contributed to consistency in accounting application in South Africa. On the advice of the panel, the listing division of JSE has issued guidance to listed companies in respect of the correct accounting treatment of certain transactions or events identified by the panel. This includes the following:

(a)   Insurance companies should not include smoothing adjustments relating to long-term investment returns in their income statements.[48]

(b)   Concerning the correct presentation in the income statement, it is inappropriate to end the income statement with the line item "headline earnings" or with any figure other than net income attributable to ordinary shareholders (the previous format of the income statement).[49]

(c)   A statement that "certain comparative figures have been restated to comply with current year classification" should be supported by full disclosure on a line-by-line basis of all reclassifications.[50]

(d)   Companies should review their accounting treatment of their share trusts to ensure that they comply with consolidation principles.[51]

(e)   Compliance with IFRS also includes compliance with the AC 500 standards.[52]

Currently, 28 companies have been referred to the GAAP Monitoring Panel for review. Nine of these have required a review of the total financial statements, and 18 have required reviews of specific policies or line items in the interim or annual financial statements.[53] The results of the recommendations and actions taken by JSE are presented in table 1.

---

[47] Ibid.
[48] JSE (2003). Long-term investment return adjustment to income statement. JSE listing division's letter. 21 February 2003.
[49] JSE (2003). Income statement presentation. JSE listing division's letter. 12 May 2003.
[50] JSE (2003). Restatement of comparative financial information. JSE listing division's letters. 22 October 2003 and 29 December 2003.
[51] JSE (2004). Consolidation of share incentive scheme trusts. JSE listing division's letter. 16 February 2004.
[52] JSE (2005). JSE. Compliance with the AC 500 series of standards. JSE listing division's letter. 24 January 2005.
[53] SAICA (2007). Summary of matters. Available from www.saica.co.za/documents (accessed 23 April 2007).

Table 1. Decisions on cases referred to the GAAP Monitoring Panel

Recommendations or actions	Number
Annual financial statements withdrawn and re-issued	3
Companies suspended (other JSE problems also present)	2
Accounting policy changed for future financial reports/other companies also adopting the policy advised to comply in the future/draft publication of the results changed before final publication of the results	7
Revised results announcement made	9
Reference to issues identified by the GAAP Monitoring Panel made in next interim results and full disclosure made in annual report	2
Correct headline earnings per share re-published on Security Exchange News Service and in annual report before distribution	1
Results revised before distribution to shareholders	2
No action required	1
Pending	1
Total	**28**

Source: SAICA (2007). *Summary of matters.* Available from www.saica.co.za.

The South African history of a lack of legal enforcement of financial reporting standards has created the opportunity for different interpretations and applications in practice, sometimes even for accounting manipulation. The lesson learned is that if South Africa truly wants to be a player in the global market, monitoring and enforcement must be a cornerstone of the financial reporting system. The IASB is not responsible for monitoring and enforcement of IFRS. These tasks are the responsibility of national regulators. South African regulators are committed to carrying rigorous monitoring and enforcement. In this respect, efforts so far have proved to be successful in ensuring compliance. Professor Harvey Wainer, chairman of the GAAP Monitoring Panel, stresses the urgency and seriousness with which the panel views its task as advisor to JSE in the achievement of this compliance.[54]

E. Involvement of local firms

The technical partners' forum in South Africa plays an important role in identifying different practices and applications of financial reporting standards. This technical partners' forum represents a network of technical partners in South Africa. This could be seen as a first step in the process of creating consistency in the application of financial reporting standards in South Africa. Through their international networks, these partners also obtain knowledge of international practices to resolve identified issues. In the sustainability of consistent global reporting practices, this networking is seen to be crucial.

---

[54] SIACA (2006). GAAP Monitoring Panel has taken a closer look at 30 listed companies. Press release. 29 November 2006; only 28 of the 30 companies have been actioned.

Local auditing firms are also required to refer accounting issues to their international desks in order to create consistency in practice. The downside, however, is increased cost and increased turn-around time, which has frustrated auditors and clients in practice.

IV. Technical and application issues

The major technical and application issues encountered in the transition to IFRS in South Africa are highlighted in this chapter. These issues have been identified through a review of the formal process of the Accounting Practices Committee and discussions with industry leaders.

A. Impairment of debtors' book

Processes to create provisions for doubtful debts were identified as an implementation issue in the second Ernst and Young survey (discussed above). The issue started in the banking industry with the adoption of the South African version of the original IAS 39 in 2001/2002.[55] At that stage, the South African Reserve Bank (the regulator of South African banks) required banks to calculate the impairment on loans and receivables on the basis of a provision matrix. This matrix did not explicitly consider a discounted cash-flow model based on expected cash flows, as required by the original IAS 39. The practical question raised at that stage was whether any adjustments to the expected cash-flow model should be made to the opening balance of retained earnings. SAICA's response was that the transitional provisions provided for an adjustment to the opening balance of retained earnings if the provisioning matrix did not explicitly consider the amount or timing of underlying cash flows.[56]

This clearly demonstrates that the adoption of IFRS for financial statement purposes is a move away from any requirements prescribed by a local regulatory body.

The second issue with the impairment of the debtors' book arose with the revision of IAS 39, through which the "expected cash-flow model" was replaced by an "incurred-loss model". The critical question was how to apply the historical loss experience test in collective assessments. The banking sector started its discussions before the IAS 39 amendment to the "incurred-loss model" was implemented and through the banking association corresponded with IFRIC. The banking sector's concerns were incorporated in the "incurred-loss model" amendment, which resulted in the sector accepting the change to the "incurred-loss model".[57]

B. Operating leases

In respect of the straight-lining of operating leases, the South African practice differed from international practice. The South African practice was that operating lease agreements with inflation escalations should not be straight-lined. It was believed that inflation escalations were "another systematic basis" from which to spread the lease payments over the term of the lease. This issue was referred to IFRIC, but the body rejected the issue on the grounds that the standard is clear: IAS 17 (leases) refers to "another systematic basis" that is "more representative of the time pattern of the user's benefit". The time pattern of the user's benefit should only be affected by factors that impact on the physical usage of the asset, which does not include inflation.

---

[55] SAICA (2001). AC 133 – Financial Instruments: Recognition and Measurement. April 2001.

[56] SAICA (2003). Circular 6/03 – Implementation Guidance for AC 133 – Financial Instruments: Recognition and Measurement. November 2003.

[57] Information obtained from discussions held with the banking sector.

SAICA issued two circulars to announce the conversion of the South African practice to the international practice.[58] In spite of many negative reactions by preparers, this diverse practice has been amended in South Africa.

C. South African dividends tax

A dual tax system for companies was introduced by the South African Income Tax Act, 1993, comprising a normal tax levied on taxable income and a secondary tax on companies (STC). STC is a tax levied on dividends declared by South African companies and is based on the amount by which a declared dividend exceeds dividends previously received. Since this is a South African-specific issue, the APB issued South African GAAP Standard AC 501 (secondary tax on companies) to clarify the accounting treatment of STC on the basis of the principles of IAS 12 on income taxes.[59]

The main question raised by AC 501 is whether STC should be included in the income-tax line in the income statement. The consensus reached was that STC is a tax on income since STC is a tax on companies and not a withholding tax. AC 501 links the recognition of the STC liability to the recognition of the liability for the dividend declared. The STC liability should be recognized when the liability for the dividend declared is recognized. AC 501 also adopted the principles of the creation of deferred assets in IAS 12. Deferred tax for an STC credit (instances where dividends received exceed dividends paid) may only be recognized to the extent that it is probable that the company would declare dividends in the future to use the STC credit.

This issue demonstrated that legislation could cover local issues not specifically covered by IFRS.

D. Black economic empowerment

Black economic empowerment (BEE) is a formal process followed in South Africa to uplift black South Africans.[60] The accounting issue in South Africa deals with the situation where entities issue equity instruments to black South Africans or entities controlled by black South Africans at a discount to fair value to achieve targets for the empowerment of black people. In terms of guidance in IFRIC 8 on scope of IFRS 2 it is clear that IFRS 2 on share-based payment applies to such BEE transactions where the fair value of cash and other assets received from BEE partners is less than the fair value of equity instruments granted to the BEE partner, i.e. the BEE equity credential element.

APB issued AC 503 (accounting for BEE) transactions to clarify whether a BEE equity credential should be recognized as an intangible asset or as an expense.[61] The conclusion reached is that BEE equity credentials should be expensed, except where the cost of the BEE equity credentials is directly attributable to the acquisition of another intangible asset. The main reason for expensing the BEE equity credentials, based on the principles of IAS 38 on intangible assets, is that the BEE equity credentials are not controlled by the entity because the entity is not able to

---

[58] SAICA (2005). Circular 7/05 – Operation Leases; and SIACA 2006: Circular 12/06 – Operating Leases. August 2006.

[59] AC 501 was effective from financial years starting on 1 January 2004.

[60] The South African Government has issued various BEE documents, including the Broad Based Black Economic Empowerment Act, Act no. 53 of 2003. The act empowers the Minister of Trade and Industry to issue codes of good practice, which are applied to determine an entity's BEE credentials.

[61] Issued in 2006.

demonstrate that it has the power to obtain the future economic benefits flowing from the underlying resource, either through legal rights or exchange transactions.

This issue regarding BEE transactions, although South African-specific, was referred to IFRIC for clarity and IFRIC issued IFRIC 8 on scope of IFRS 2 in response.

E. Divergence due to IFRIC rejecting items

Sometimes IFRIC rejects items submitted to it for consideration on the grounds that it considers the appropriate accounting treatment to be clear. However, the South African experience is that IFRIC's reasoning in such cases could identify divergence of practice in South Africa. SAICA's Circular 09/06, which relates to cash discounts, settlement discounts, other rebates and extended payment terms, contains examples where such divergence has been identified.[62]

(a) Cash discounts: IFRIC's view is that IAS 2 (inventory) provides adequate guidance. Cash discounts received should be deducted from the cost of the goods purchased. In contrast, many South African entities account for cash discounts received as "other income", thus creating divergence. Similarly, Circular 9/06 clarifies that cash discounts granted to customers should reduce the amount of revenue recognized on the date of sale.

(b) Settlement discounts: In rejecting the issue regarding settlement discounts, IFRIC agreed that settlement discounts allowed should be estimated at the time of sale and presented as a reduction in revenue. Settlement discounts received should similarly be deducted from the cost of inventory. The practice of many South African entities at the time was to account for settlement discounts allowed to customers as "operating expenses" and settlement discounts received as "other income".

(c) Other rebates: Many South African entities account for rebates received as "other income". However, IFRIC agreed that in terms of IAS 2 (inventory), those rebates that have been received as a reduction in the purchase price of inventories should be taken into account in the measurement of the cost of inventory. Rebates specifically related to selling expenses would not be deducted from the cost of inventory.

(d) Extended payment terms: There continues to be diversity in practice on the treatment of extended payment terms. This issue remains unresolved, as more than one standard deals with principles on deferred settlements, and different preparers interpret the requirements differently. IAS 2 (inventory) states that, when the arrangement effectively contains a financing element, that element must be recognized as interest over the period of the finance. IAS 18 makes a similar reference in respect of the recognition of revenue. The IFRIC reasons for rejecting an interpretation are that the accounting treatment for extended payment terms such as six-month's interest-free credit is clear: the time value of money should be reflected when it is material. The diversity has arisen with regard to the interpretation of extended credit (and therefore the necessity to present value the amounts in terms of IAS 39 (financial instruments: recognition and measurement)). Some auditors and users interpret extended credit as

---

62 SAICA (2006). Circular 09/06 – Transactions giving rise to Adjustments to Revenue/Purchases. May 2006.

payment after the transaction date (i.e. that credit has been extended) and others have interpreted it as credit being extended for a period that is longer than normal for that industry. In addition, some preparers contend that when cash sales are concluded at the same selling price as those with extended payment terms, the sales revenue to be recognized must be the same.

F. Insurance industry: anomalies relating to treasury shares

Prior to the adoption of IFRS, the insurance industry applied a local standard, which had the effect of ring-fencing the results of insurance businesses.[63] Assets and liabilities relating to insurance business were disclosed separately from other business in the financial statements. The move to IFRS and also the application of IFRS 4 on insurance contracts has resulted in assets being disclosed by their nature. For instance, financial assets held to manage the insurance business are not disclosed separately from other assets.

The main result of the abolishment of the ring-fencing principle is the effect of treasury shares. Certain insurance divisions (subsidiaries) invest in equity shares of the entity (holding company). For instance, insurance operations offer products that are linked to equity performance, and, as a result, they often invest in shares of their holding companies.[64] These shares could also be bought for the purpose of linked investments (investments linked to the performance of a basket of shares) or to generate a direct return for policyholders. The main anomaly is that the value of these shares would be considered in the value of the insurance liability, but that the effect on the asset side is eliminated through the deduction of such shares as treasury shares from equity. The treasury shares are also deducted from the weighted number of shares in issue for the earnings per share calculation, which could potentially inflate the earnings per share number on an IFRS basis.

The issue of treasury shares was discussed with Sir David Tweedie, chairman of the IASB, when he visited South Africa in November 2006. His response was that the IASB had discussed the topic at various board meetings and had not been able to arrive at an acceptable solution without creating an exception for an industry.[65]

G. Fair value measurement considerations

Another concern raised by the APB and the Accounting Practices Committee at their meeting with Sir David Tweedie was the application of fair value measurement applied to financial instruments in cases where there was no active market or where the market was illiquid.[66] The concern especially relates to instances where fair value measurement is based on management's estimates.

Tweedie's response was that an evaluation of the discussion paper on fair value measurement guidance was needed, which would contain a hierarchy for fair value measurement. This evaluation would be the process needed to resolve the fair value measurement concerns. The progress on this project is being closely monitored in South Africa.

---

[63] AC 121 – Disclosure in the Financial Statements of Long-term Insurers was abolished during 2004.

[64] SAICA (2006). Minutes of the meeting of the APC, 30 November 2006 (the meeting where the visit of Sir David Tweedie was documented).

[65] Ibid.

[66] Ibid.

H. Separate financial statements

In South Africa, holding companies were always required to prepare separate financial statements on the basis of the South African statements of GAAP. While IFRS are not explicitly written for consolidated financial statements only, there is almost an implicit focus on the consolidated position rather than the separate financial statements.[67]

Some of the challenges facing preparers of financial statements stem from the uncertainty of applying the concept of substance over legal form. In respect of special purpose entities, the question is to what extent a "look-through" approach should be applied in the separate financial statements to reflect the economic substance rather than the legal form on the basis that the special purpose entity was effectively just a conduit or a warehousing vehicle. Similarly, in respect of transactions with other related parties, the question is to what extent the economic substance, and not merely the legal form, should be analyzed and reflected, particularly where the transactions might not be on an arm's-length basis.

Sir David Tweedie's response in this regard was that the IASB was aware of these issues and had been debating them, and that the preference at this stage was for the look-through approach to be applied.[68]

V.   Conclusion

The adoption of IFRS has clearly increased South Africa's role as a global player in the accounting field and has strengthened uniformity in the application of IFRS in South Africa. Listed companies and the accounting practice have tackled the task of implementing IFRS diligently and have achieved great successes. Clearly, many teething problems have been resolved.

The adoption of IFRS has enhanced consistency of the application of IFRS and has further confirmed the need for a local technical body that will contribute to the IASB due process and resolve specific local issues and divergence in practice.

The country has witnessed a significant growth in the technical accounting departments of audit firms to cope with the increased technical demand. However, many accounting specialists trained in South Africa have left the country because of global demand for their skills.

The challenges facing South Africa are to create a process of legal backing for accounting standards by proper monitoring and enforcement structures and to implement a system of differential reporting.

---

[67] Ibid.
[68] Ibid.

Chapter IX

Case study of Turkey

I. Introduction[1]

As a developing country with an emerging capital market, Turkey closely follows developments in international financial reporting and auditing. This report presents the historical development of accounting and financial reporting in the country and discusses the recent regulatory developments following the attempts at convergence with the global set of financial reporting standards that is referred to as the international financial reporting standards (IFRS). In doing so, this report conveys the Turkish experience in adapting to IFRS as well as lessons learned in the implementation process.

Turkey has been attracting foreign direct investment (FDI) at various levels since the establishment of the Turkish Republic in 1923. Turkish companies started to invest in other countries in the late 1990s. The amount of FDI flowing into Turkey between 2002 and 2005 was $15.4 billion, whereas FDI flowing out of Turkey during the same period was $2.6 billion.[2] As of 31 December 2006, there were 14,932 companies in Turkey with foreign capital. Five percent of these companies received investments from the United States, and 56 per cent received investments from European Union-based companies.[3] Turkish companies, on the other hand, had most of their investments in the European Union and in the Commonwealth of the Independent States.

Turkey was hit by a severe economic crisis in November 2000 that continued until February 2001. There was a 7.5 per cent contraction in gross domestic product (GDP) and inflation jumped, with an annual increase in the consumer price index of 68.5 per cent. Economic growth recovered in the following years and inflation fell below 10 per cent starting in 2004. The GDP growth rate for 2006 was 6.1 per cent, reaching $400 billion.[4]

Turkey applied for membership in the European Union in 1999, and is currently a candidate country. With the resolution adopted by the European Parliament on 15 December 2004, negotiations for full membership started on 3 October 2005. Among many other legislative issues, the relations with the European Union require Turkey to adapt its financial reporting system to European Union legislation.

---

[1] This chapter was prepared and edited by the UNCTAD secretariat with substantive inputs from Professor F.N. Can ı mga-Mu an of Middle East Technical University–Ankara and Nazlı Ho al-Akman of Bilkent University–Ankara.

[2] www.unctad.org.

[3] www.hazine.gov.tr.

[4] siteresources.worldbank.org, www.turkstat.gov.tr, www.turkisheconomy.org.uk.

A brief history of accounting in Turkey[5]

The development of accounting practices in Turkey is heavily influenced by the practices of a number of Western countries as a result of the economic and political ties in a specific period. The first Commercial Code of 1850 was a translation of the French Commercial Code and reflected the French influence of the era. The end of the nineteenth century and the beginning of the twentieth century mark the increased trade relations between Turkey and Europe, especially Germany.

These historical and political developments – and the fact that most foreign manufacturing businesses had been operated by Germans at the start of the Turkish Republic – led to strong German influence on the economic development of the emerging State. Following the establishment of the Turkish Republic in 1923, a second Commercial Code was enacted in 1926 (Act No. 826). This code was based on the German commerce and company laws that controlled the accounting rules.

As a result of the lack of private enterprises and private capital at the beginning of the republic, the State took the responsibility to set up heavy industry and several manufacturing companies. These State-founded and operated companies are called State economic enterprises (SEEs), and Sümerbank (mine and textile products) was founded as the first SEE in 1933. It was originally entrusted with the operation of principal mines that were acquired through nationalization from German companies. Therefore, it is not surprising to see that Sümerbank's and other SEEs' accounting systems were developed by experts from Germany. Hence, through these enterprises, the German influence was carried to the private sector as well. Furthermore, in the late 1930s, Turkey welcomed German academics of various fields in Turkish universities.

The decade 1950–1960 marks the first attempts towards a more liberal economy. The current Commercial Code of 1956 came into effect on 1 January 1957, following contemporary economic developments.

After the Second World War, developments in the world economy such as the Bretton Woods economic conference affected the Turkish economy. In 1950, the Turkish Industrial Development Bank was founded with support from the World Bank to foster and finance private industrial investments. In the early 1950s, the country enjoyed unprecedented economic growth. The economic boom ended in the mid-1950s, and was followed by a period of economic crisis. A major outcome of the crisis was the need for foreign loans that eventually led to a stabilization programme headed by the International Monetary Fund in 1958[6].

During the 1950s, incentives were provided for the private sector and foreign investments. Since the second half of that decade, American expertise has been utilized, and the Turkish economic system has thus been heavily influenced by the American system. Successful individuals in various fields have been trained, and have pursued graduate degrees in foreign countries, especially in the United States of America, starting in the late 1950s. Since the return of the first of these graduates in the early 1960s, the accounting system has been heavily influenced by the American system. Furthermore, the American influence was also felt in the curriculum of business schools, especially in the fields of management and accounting.

---

[5] This section is adapted from the article: Simga-Mugan C and Hosal-Akman N (2005). Convergence to international financial reporting standards: The case of Turkey. *International Journal of Accounting, Auditing and Performance Evaluation.* Vol. 2, No. 1/2: 12–139.

[6] Ceyhun F (1992). Turkey's debt crises in historical perspective: A critical analysis. *METU Studies in Development.* Vol.19, No.1: 9–49.

The decade 1970–1980 was an era of political instability which, together with the oil crises in 1973 and 1974, had adverse effects on the Turkish economy. From 1977 onwards, Turkey faced great difficulties in meeting foreign debt payments and encountered import bottlenecks. The increase in the wholesale price index reached 63.9 per cent per annum in 1979 and 107.2 per cent per annum in 1980.[7]

In January 1980, a series of economic decisions following the International Monetary Fund's recommendations were taken to reduce the inflation rate, increase production, and support importing activities. In the reconstruction period starting in the early 1980s, Act No. 2499 was put into effect in 1981 by the Parliament to prepare the grounds for establishing the Capital Markets Board (CMB) and was amended in 2002. The Istanbul Stock Exchange (ISE) law was adopted in 1984, but full operations did not start until 1986. It is still the only stock exchange in Turkey. FDI rules were eased in 1988 and 1989.

Foundation of the CMB, ISE and the increase in foreign investments promoted the development of accounting and auditing standards. Increases in joint ventures and foreign trade led to the establishment of offices by the then "Big Eight" accounting firms in Turkey. As a result of these developments, large private enterprises started to report their financial statements in accordance with the International Accounting Standards (IAS), in addition to national reporting requirements. During this decade, Turkey enjoyed economic growth.

Turkey started the 1990s on a sound economic footing. However, overall it was an economically unstable decade. The first major crisis was in 1994. This was followed by further crises in 1997, 1998 and 1999. During this decade, the inflation rate surpassed 100 per cent. As a result of the instability and high inflation rates, historical financial statements lost their information value. Although IAS had been translated into Turkish since the beginning of 1980s by the Turkish Expert Accountants' Association, they were not enforced by any authority.[8] Companies did not use inflation accounting. The subsidiaries of multinational companies and joint venture companies were applying inflation accounting either voluntarily or when it was required by the headquarters of the parent company.

In line with European Union requirements, the CMB issued the IFRS-based standard Communiqué Serial: XI, No. 25, entitled "Accounting Standards in Capital Markets", on 15 November 2003 (from then on the new CMB rules) and required publicly owned and traded companies to use the new rules starting January 2005, while encouraging early adoption. Currently, there are 333 companies traded on the ISE, while 65 companies are traded on foreign stock exchanges, including Frankfurt, London, and New York.[9] For companies traded on European Union stock exchanges, IFRS-based statements are required, which is also allowed by the CMB. However, at present, there are no foreign companies listed on the Istanbul Stock Exchange.

II. Regulatory framework

A. Non-bank private entities

Until the establishment of the CMB and the ISE, legal requirements were the main influence on the financial accounting system. Consequently, the Procedural Tax Code heavily influenced accounting practice in Turkey.

---

[7] Simga-Mugan C (1995). Accounting in Turkey. *The European Accounting Review*. Vol. 4, No.2: 351–371.
[8] http://www.tmud.org.tr/default.asp.
[9] www.reuters.com (found under TRSTOKS).

The first set of financial accounting standards was developed in January 1989 by the CMB to be in effect for the fiscal years that started on or after 1 January 1989 (Serial X, No. 11).[10]

As mentioned above, the environment surrounding the accounting practice in Turkey went through several transformations. However, accounting principles did not show such a development, and accounting was, and to some extent still is, treated as identical to tax accounting. Moreover, although there have been several attempts to form an accounting body since the 1940s, until recently there was no effort to pursue the establishment of standards. The main reason for this delay is the lack of pressure on Turkish companies to make publicly available comparable financial statements, because most of the businesses are family-owned. The accountants in such companies are responsible for (1) bookkeeping for tax purposes (i.e. following procedural tax code); (2) cash management; (3) budgeting; (4) preparation of tax returns and financial statements required by the tax codes; and (5) very limited internal auditing.

In 1992, the Ministry of Finance organized a committee to establish accounting principles and a uniform chart of accounts that would be used by all companies. The ministry published the committee's report in a communiqué on 26 December 1992 establishing the principles and the Turkish Uniform Chart of Accounts (TUCA) to take effect 1 January 1994. All companies except banks, brokerage firms and insurance companies are required to conform to the guidelines stated in the communiqué.

According to the requirements of the 1992 communiqué, financial statements prepared in Turkey include a balance sheet, an income statement, a statement of cost of goods sold, a funds flow statement, a cash flow statement, a profit distribution statement and a statement of owners' equity, as well as notes to these statements. The balance sheet, income statement and notes to these statements constitute the fundamental statements, and the others are supplementary statements. The Ministry of Finance communiqué of September 1994 states that small companies are required to submit the fundamental statements only. Tax rules, on the other hand, require a balance sheet and an income statement from all first-class merchants. Financial statements have to be prepared within the three months following the end of an accounting period, which is usually the year end.

The Code of Obligations and the Commercial Code regulate the formation and activities of the businesses. The Code of Obligations controls ordinary partnerships which lack the status of legal entity. The Commercial Code, on the other hand, specifies the following types of legal entities:

(a) General and special partnerships;

(b) Limited partnerships;

(c) Partnerships limited by shares; and

(d) Corporations.

As mentioned above, the CMB issued the first financial accounting standards for publicly owned companies in 1989, following the inauguration of the ISE in 1986. This set of CMB standards was comparable to IAS, including the assumptions of going concern, consistency, time period, unit of measure and the basic principles such as, cost, matching, conservatism, materiality, objectivity and full disclosure. However, there were very significant differences in measurement and disclosure issues. The significant differences, among others, were accounting

---

[10] www.spk.gov.tr.

for the effects of inflation under hyperinflationary economies, and also accounting for long-term investments. Although Turkey had been experiencing considerable rates of inflation since 1984, financial statements were prepared at historical cost except for the revaluation of property, plant and equipment. Furthermore, long-term investments including subsidiaries and equity participations were carried at cost.

If the number of shareholders of a corporation exceeds 250, then that corporation is categorized as a publicly-owned company and is subject to CMB regulations. Currently, there are 274 publicly-owned companies whose securities are not publicly traded. Serial X, No. 11 standards (old CMB rules) are still in effect to regulate financial reporting of such entities. Publicly owned companies whose shares are traded in the stock exchange are subject to the new CMB rules (Serial X, No. 25) that are based on IFRS.

There are some major issues that are covered in IFRS/IAS but not in the old CMB rules. These can be summarized as follows:

(a) Impairment of assets (IAS 36);

(b) The de-recognition of financial assets (IAS 39);

(c) Provision for employee benefits other than lump-sum termination indemnities (IAS 19);

(d) Segment reporting (IAS 14);

(e) Provisions, contingent liabilities and contingent assets (IAS 37);

(f) Deferred taxes (IAS 12);

(g) Treasury shares (IAS 32); and

(h) Hedge accounting (IAS 39).

Furthermore, there are certain differences between the old CMB rules and IFRS/IAS that could lead to reporting of different financial results and financial position. Major differences include:

(a) Measurement issues:

(i) According to CMB rules, foreign exchange losses that arise from acquisition of property, plant and equipment can be capitalized after related assets are put into use. IFRS and IAS, on the other hand, require recording of such foreign exchange losses as period expenses.

(ii) CMB rules require that construction contracts should be accounted for using the completed contract method, whereas IFRS and IAS require the use of percentage of completion or cost recovery methods.

(iii) Although IFRS and IAS treat organization and research costs as period expenses while permitting capitalization of development costs under special circumstances, CMB rules allow for capitalization of organization, research and development costs.

(iv) The amortization period of goodwill is different between the two sets of standards.

(v) While IFRS and IAS require discounting of the pension obligations to present value, CMB rules do not impose such a requirement.

(vi) All types of leases are accounted for as operating leases according to

CMB rules.

(b) Disclosure issues:

(i) According to the CMB rules the applicability of related parties is limited to shareholders, subsidiary and equity investments whereas related parties are more broadly defined in IFRS/IAS.

(ii) There are no specific disclosure requirements relating to the fair value of financial assets and liabilities except for marketable securities under the CMB rules.

(iii) Statement of changes in shareholders' equity is not required by the CMB rules.

(iv) CMB rules on format of the statement of cash flows do not require a breakdown of cash flows by type of activity.

In November 2003, the CMB issued a communiqué to adapt the financial reporting standards of traded companies in ISE to IAS and IFRS (Series XI, No. 25). The standards were mandatory for all publicly traded companies and intermediary institutions (brokerage firms) from the beginning of 2005. The new standards in the communiqué are essentially the same as IAS/IFRS except for the amendments by the IASB after 2004. One of the differences between the new CMB rules and IFRS lies in the treatment of goodwill. According to CMB rules, goodwill is still amortized.

According to tax rules, on the other hand, in principle, accrual accounting is required, but the treatment of certain items is closer to cash accounting. At the same time, with the CMB, the Ministry of Finance required a one-time application of inflation accounting to restate the balance sheet ending 31 December 2003 or at the end of the then current fiscal year.[11]

Through Act No. 4487 dated December 1999, an addendum was made to the Capital Markets Act establishing the Turkish Accounting Standards Board to issue Turkish accounting standards that would facilitate fair disclosure of financial position. The board has both administrative and financial autonomy. It held its first meeting in March 2002, and has nine representatives from the Ministry of Finance, Higher Education Council, the CMB, the Under-Secretariat of Treasury, Ministry of Industry and Commerce, the Banking Regulation and Supervision Agency (BRSA), the Union of Chambers and Commodity Exchanges in Turkey, a self-employed accountant and a certified financial consultant from Union of Certified Public Accountants and Sworn-in Certified Public Accountants in Turkey.[12]

The Turkish Accounting Standards Board has an agreement with the IASB to officially translate and publish IFRS/IAS and the related interpretations. As of mid-2007, the Turkish Accounting Standards Board had issued 31 Turkish accounting standards and seven Turkish financial reporting standards. All of these issued standards correspond to the respective IAS and IFRS.

Currently, the Turkish Accounting Standards Board has no enforcement authority to require any Turkish company to prepare financial statements in accordance with Turkish accounting standards or Turkish financial reporting standards (hereinafter referred to as Turkish accounting standards).

---

[11] Simga-Mugan and Akman N (2002). Turkey. Revised chapter in World Accounting, Release 24. Orsini L et al. (eds). Lexis-Nexis/Matthew-Bender, November.

[12] www.turmob.org.tr.

Consolidation rules are not required under the present Commercial Code and tax legislation. However, the CMB issued a communiqué in 2003 (Serial XI, No. 21) that stipulates consolidation of financial position of companies that meet the criteria which are the same as IFRS rules for publicly owned companies whose shares are traded. Since adoption of new IFRS-based CMB rules, companies are required to comply with the new regulation. The Turkish Accounting Standards Board also published Turkish accounting standard 27 on consolidated and separate financial statement, which is fully compatible with IAS 27.

Another major discrepancy between the tax rules and the accounting rules concerns fixed assets. According to the accounting rules, the cost of fixed assets includes – in addition to the acquisition cost – items such as interest expense on self-constructed assets (capitalized until the asset is ready for use), foreign exchange losses on the purchase price of the assets, the debts incurred for such assets, and long-term investments (capitalized until the debt for the asset or investment is paid in full). According to tax rules, however, companies may continue to capitalize the interest expense related to loans used to finance such assets after the asset is in use.

According to both the old CMB regulations and the Ministry of Finance requirements between 1983 and 2003, companies revalued their fixed assets (except land) and the related accumulated depreciation if they wished, provided that they have been using those fixed assets for more than one year. The revaluation rate was based on an index published by the Ministry of Finance every December that approximated the country's annual inflation rate. The difference between the net revalued fixed assets of the current period (revalued cost minus revalued accumulated depreciation) and the previous period was accumulated under the owners' equity section of the balance sheet under the name "revaluation fund". This revaluation surplus was non-taxable unless distributed, and may have been added to capital via issuance of bonus (free) shares. With the inception of inflation accounting in 2003, this practice was abandoned.

B. Banks and financial institutions

Financial reporting of financial institutions is regulated by BRSA. Until recently, BRSA issued its own set of accounting standards that financial institutions had to comply with. However, since November 2006, these institutions have been required to apply Turkish accounting standards to prepare their financial statements, except for certain differences such as loan loss provisions.

In summary, financial reporting in Turkey has a multi-institutional structure. Turkish companies prepare their financial reports according to different sets of accounting standards, depending on the nature of their business and their shareholding structure. Table 1 summarizes the reporting requirements of different companies.

Table 1. Reporting requirements of different companies

Publicly owned but not traded in the stock exchange	Old CMB standards (Series XI, No. 1 and its amendments)
Publicly owned and traded in the stock exchange	New CMB standards (Series XI, No. 25 and its amendments)
Brokerage companies	New CMB standards (Series XI, No. 25 and its amendments)
Banks and financial institutions	Turkish accounting standards
Insurance companies	Communiqué of under secretariat of treasury

As illustrated in the table above, presently companies that are not publicly owned are not required to apply any accounting standards other than Ministry of Finance's communiqué of 1992 and the tax legislation.

C. The accounting profession and auditing

The accounting profession was formally defined by Act No. 3968, enacted in 1989. The three categories of accountants according to the law are as follows:

(a) Independent accountant: The independent accountant is a practising accountant who may keep the accounting records of companies and develop accounting systems within the companies.

(b) Certified public accountant: Apart from the responsibilities of independent accountants, certified public accountants may conduct audits and perform consulting services.

(c) Sworn-in certified public accountant: Sworn-in certified public accountants may not keep accounting records for their clients. They have the responsibility of certifying the financial statements as defined by the law.

The law also defines the competencies that are required (education, certificates and diplomas) to become an independent accountant, a certified public accountant and a sworn-in certified public accountant. The professionals are recognized by the Turkish Union of Chambers of Certified Public Accountants and are sworn in as such.

The chambers of certified public accountants and sworn-in certified public accountants are separate. Chambers are professional organizations regarded as legal entities carrying qualities of public institutions. They are established to meet the needs of members of the profession, facilitate their professional activities, develop the profession in compliance with common requirements, maintain professional discipline and ethics, and ensure the prevalence of honesty and mutual confidence in the work of the members of the profession and in their relations with their clients.

Auditing activities and audit firms in capital markets are regulated by the CMB (Communiqué Serial: X, No. 22). Existing CMB regulations have been revised following regulatory reforms that were passed in the United States and the European Union. These include:

(a) Separation of audit and consultancy;

(b) Establishment of audit committees for companies whose securities are publicly traded and for brokerage firms;

(c) Audit firm rotation; and

(d) Determination of responsibility for the preparation, presentation and accuracy of financial statements and annual reports.

An audit firm can audit a company whose securities are publicly traded for a maximum of seven years. At the end of seven years of service, the audit of that company should be contracted to another audit firm. In order for the first auditing firm to resume the auditing services of the same company, at least two accounting periods should elapse.

Under CMB rules, in order to conduct auditing activities, an auditing firm should meet the following requirements:

(a) An audit firm should be incorporated as a corporation with shares written to the name.

(b) The major partner should own 51 per cent of the shares;

(c) Auditors should be university graduates in the fields of economics and business administration.

(d) The firm should only be engaged in auditing activities.

(e) The firm should be insured (new amendment in 2007).

As noted above, banks and financial institutions are regulated by BRSA, and this agency thus oversees independent audit processes of such institutions. BRSA authorizes and terminates the activities of the audit companies. It carries out these activities through two by-laws: the law on independent audit of banks and authorization of independent audit firms.

The information technologies auditing project started in 2004 with a change in the by-laws of BRSA which resulted in a partial reorganization of the agency. A working group was established that studied the relevant standards and literature. In addition, a survey on the technical capacity of the banks was carried out around the same time. Lastly, in May 2006, BRSA issued a communiqué on auditing of information technologies of banks (IT audit). It adopted the Control Objectives for Information and Related Technology (COBIT).[13]

III. Capacity-building

In code law countries, such as Turkey, standard-setting and enforcement are primarily functions of government institutions. In such countries, there is a lower demand for high-quality financial reporting and disclosure, as the reporting model is oriented towards tax offices and financial institutions. In common law countries, on the other hand, the enforcement of high-quality financial reporting standards is needed for shareholder protection.

Therefore, in Turkey, issuing accounting standards is not enough for enforcement of those standards. Legally, companies should be required to use Turkish accounting standards for those IFRS-compatible standards to be fully enforced.

A new draft commercial code that will introduce new financial reporting requirements as required by Turkish accounting standards has been discussed in the relevant commissions of the Parliament since the beginning of 2007. However, it is not expected to be enacted before 2008. Article 64 of the draft code requires all companies excluding small and medium-sized enterprises (SMEs) to prepare financial statements in accordance with Turkish accounting standards. Developing accounting standards for SMEs is an ongoing project of the Turkish Accounting Standards Board. These standards are expected to be a simplified version of Turkish accounting standards which would be in line with the IASB SME project.

The dilemma of preparing financial statements per tax requirements or according to accounting standards was also apparent in the responses of the executives who participated in a survey that assessed the perceptions of the preparers regarding IFRS.[14] Eighteen per cent of the respondents see the differences between the IFRS-based standards and tax regulations as a major obstacle in applying the standards.

Therefore, in Turkey, standards alone do not guarantee the quality of financial information disclosed, rather the institutional factors such as the incentive of preparers should be considered.

---

[13] www.bddk.org.tr.

[14] Akman N, Simga-Mugan C, Arikboga D (2005). *Awaiting IFRS: Perceptions and Demands of Executives In An Emerging Market.* Accounting Academician's Collaboration Foundation of Turkey, second Annual Accounting Conference. 10–12 November 2005. Istanbul.

The accounting managers of publicly owned companies are already familiar with IAS-based accounting standards. However, most of the accounting managers of family-owned businesses are not exposed to such standards and are not familiar with the content of Turkish accounting standards. Once the draft commercial code is enacted and companies start to apply Turkish accounting standards, these managers will be in extremely difficult positions with respect to preparing financial statements. Family-owned companies comprise more than 85 per cent of businesses in Turkey.

Training and education on IFRS are mostly provided by universities and academic organizations. Universities already incorporated IFRS courses in their graduate and undergraduate curriculums as elective courses. In some universities, the principles of accounting courses are covered using IFRS. Accounting textbooks are revised to reflect the changes that are brought about by the implementation of IFRS.

One of the academic organizations, the Accounting Academicians' Collaboration Foundation, organizes international and national seminars and workshops open to practitioners and academicians on various issues of IFRS/Turkish accounting standards (such as implementation of IAS 39).[15] Similarly, the Turkish Expert Accountants' Association holds seminars on IFRS in general, and on some specific standards.[16]

In order to align auditing standards with international developments, the CMB published revised auditing rules and regulations by Communiqué Serial X, No. 22 in 2006 and later amended it with No. 23 in 2007. This communiqué states that:

"Independent auditing firms, their auditors and other staff shall not provide any issuer or intermediary, contemporaneously with the audit, any non-audit service, with or without fee, including:

    (a) Bookkeeping and other related services;

    (b) Financial information systems design and implementation;

    (c) Services on management, accounting and finance;

    (d) Appraisal or valuation services and actuarial services;

    (e) Internal audit outsourcing services;

    (f) Legal services and expert services;

    (g) Any other consultation services."

As mentioned in the Report on the Observance of Standards and Codes of the World Bank, the Turkish Auditing Standards Board was formed in 2003.[17] It issues national auditing standards which in essence are translations of IAS issued by the International Auditing and Assurance Standards Board of the International Federation of Accountants. However, before the new commercial code is enacted, there is no requirement for companies other than entities whose shares are publicly traded to have their financial statements audited.

In addition to accounting and auditing standards, the CMB initiated the Corporate Governance Code. This code is based on Organization for Economic Cooperation and Development principles, and requires publicly traded companies to publish their corporate

---

[15] www.modav.org.tr.

[16] www.tmud.org.tr.

[17] www.imf.org.

governance ratings. Rating agencies can rate the level of compliance of companies with corporate governance practices recommended by the Capital Markets Board of Turkey.

IV. Lessons learned

Turkey is one of the proactive countries that took steps to improve its financial reporting and auditing system to align the requirements with the commencement of IFRS in 2005.

In essence, the adoption of IFRS-based standards turned out to be a three-step process where the first step was the early adoption of IFRS between 2003 and 2005 by companies whose shares are publicly traded. The second step was the compulsory adoption of IFRS starting in 2005, again by the traded companies. The third step was the mandatory adoption by all publicly owned companies upon the enactment of the draft commercial code.

Encouraging the traded companies to adopt IFRS or IFRS-based CMB standards before 2005 led to two benefits:

(a) More transparent financial statements were introduced; and

(b) The experience of the early adopters during the transition period helped the other publicly traded companies.

The adoption of IFRS-based rules by the traded companies before the other private companies will ease the way for the latter companies. Non-publicly-owned private companies will benefit from their publicly traded counterparts' experience during the implementation.

Turkish accounting standards will affect many parties covering both the internal and external users of financial statements. For external users such as foreign and domestic stock investors, Turkish accounting standards will bring transparency and comparability. These users will find themselves at ease while making investment decisions with the help of comparable and consistent financial data.

A study[18] examining the market reaction to inflation accounting-based financial reports indicated that accounting earnings announcements have an effect on market prices at a 0.10 significance level. It also found that inflation-adjusted financial reports had an impact on abnormal returns during the event window surrounding the annual earnings announcements. The paired samples T-test performed included 36 pairs of cumulative standardized abnormal return data for 2002 and 2004. The test results showed that, at a 95 per cent confidence level, the hypothesis that these two samples have equal means was rejected. This implies that the market reacted to inflation-adjusted data.

One of the urgent issues in Turkey is to solve the multi-institutional structure of the accounting environment. There should be one accounting standard-setting body for all entities.

A related issue is the enforcement of Turkish accounting standards. Until the draft commercial code is enacted, the Turkish Accounting Standards Board does not have any power to enforce the adoption of Turkish accounting standards by all companies. As stated above, BRSA is the only authority that requires the use of Turkish accounting standards. It could be beneficial for the CMB and Under-Secretariat of Treasury to follow the BRSA example and entrust their standard-setting authority to the Turkish Accounting Standards Board.

---

[18] An ongoing study being carried by Professor F., Can ı mga-Mu an et al. at the Middle East Technical University, Ankara

Significant amounts of training and education for financial statement preparers and small and local auditing companies are needed. A lesson learned from the initial implementation is the insufficient understanding of accounting standards by these groups.

Generally, accounting standards do not address the full details of application that requires judgment from the management of entities. Turkish accounting standards involve a great deal of management judgment. As significant judgment is exercised in applying the accounting standards, incomplete comprehension of standards would lead to lower-quality financial information.

The results obtained through the survey discussed above highlighted the inadequate level of understanding of the accounting standards by financial-statement preparers. As the demand for independent auditors will increase upon the enactment of the draft commercial code, there should be enough training for the professional accountants and auditors with respect to both accounting and auditing standards.

Within this framework, the results of the Turkish survey with respect to the question of the sources of advisory services (or consulting services) for the implementation of the IFRS-based accounting standards points to a very important potential problem of infringement of independence of audit companies. It should be noted that a majority of the respondents indicated that they intend to ask for consultancy from their current auditors, although such a practice is forbidden by CMB regulations.

The proposed changes in disclosure and particularly in measurement issues stated above will bring additional responsibilities to auditing firms, which are expected to be knowledgeable on the new set of accounting rules. There are indications that finance executives and accounting department staff will need extensive training on the application of Turkish accounting standards.

CMB and the Turkish Accounting Standards Board should jointly establish a technical inquiry service for companies and auditors to answer very specific questions coming from the users of the accounting standards, and based on the common questions and complaints develop recommendations to the Turkish Accounting Standards Board.

There are currently private training programmes that are available to the public. Especially in cases where these programmes are offered by spin-offs of the auditing firms, conflict of interest might be a problem which could result in ethical dilemmas. Thus, the Turkish Accounting Standards Board should oversee and regulate the content of these programmes and closely monitor the auditor/client relationship.

The Turkish Accounting Standards Board has already translated IASB interpretations. However, these interpretations might not adequately address the concerns within the Turkish context. Therefore, the board should establish an interpretations committee to resolve national and when necessary sector-specific issues that may come up during the implementation of Turkish accounting standards. This committee should also publish books on the application of various standards.

One of the basic objectives of the IASB is "to bring about convergence of national accounting standards and International Accounting Standards and International Financial Reporting Standards to high-quality solutions".[19] It might be beneficial if the Turkish Accounting Standards Board communicates to the IASB the concerns and questions of the Turkish practice, along with the solutions provided. Such an effort could assist Turkey as well as other developing countries in aligning their national standards with IFRS.

---

[19] www.iasb.org.

Currently, there is no supervision of auditing companies as a whole. The CMB carries out inspections to determine whether auditing companies are performing their audit engagements in accordance with auditing standards. There should be a public oversight board to supervise the implementation of auditing standards and make sure that auditing companies are acting with due care. While the establishment of a public oversight board has been discussed since 2004, no legal or regulatory action has yet been taken.

V. Conclusion

Over the years, the Turkish accounting system has undergone considerable change. Financial accounting and reporting started as a record-keeping for tax purposes. Although Turkey could still be classified as a code law country, since the 1960s there is a trend toward Anglo-Saxon-style reporting. This movement accelerated after the establishment of ISE. The growth of global trade and investment also accelerated the change in accounting and auditing standards. As a result, Turkey accepted to adopt the IFRS by translating them into Turkish. Similarly, International Standards on Auditing have also been translated and put into effect.

In code law countries such as Turkey, laws need to be changed in order to enforce an accounting standard. The Turkish experience regarding the process of enacting the new commercial code is an excellent example. Well-known lawyers and accountants from the country have been working on the draft code for more than six years. Therefore, countries that intend to implement IFRS should have their transition plans ready well ahead of launching IFRS.

At present, Turkey faces two main obstacles. The first one relates to endowing the Turkish Accounting Standards Board with enforcement authority; the second one to the training of the accountants and staff of the local auditing firms.

The Turkish experience on the way to converge with the international accounting and auditing standards could help other developing countries with respect to the following issues:

(a) It might be better to require the use of IFRS or IFRS-based national standards in the case of large companies that could already be familiar with the international accounting standards to some extent.

(b) It would be helpful to have a single authority that oversees the development and implementation of the standards.

(c) It would be advisable to train the trainers before launching the accounting and auditing standards.